JUST TESTING

by the same author

GOSHAWK SQUADRON
THE ELDORADO NETWORK
PIECE OF CAKE

Just Testing

DEREK ROBINSON

COLLINS HARVILL
8 Grafton Street London W1
1985

William Collins Sons & Co. Ltd
London · Glasgow · Sydney · Auckland
Toronto · Johannesburg

British Library Cataloguing in Publication Data
Robinson, Derek
  Just Testing.
  1. Atomic bomb —— Great Britain —— Testing ——
  Hygienic aspects —— History
  I. Title
  358'.39   UG1282.A8

ISBN 0-00-272335-2

First published by Collins Harvill 1985
© Derek Robinson 1985

Photoset in Linotron Sabon by
Rowland Phototypesetting Ltd, Bury St Edmunds, Suffolk
Printed in Great Britain by
Billings & Sons Ltd, Worcester

CONTENTS

INTRODUCTION

This book is about the twenty thousand British servicemen who worked at the sites where British nuclear weapons were tested in the 1950s, and who witnessed those tests. They served at Maralinga and Emu in South Australia, at the Monte Bello Islands off Western Australia, and at Christmas and Malden Islands thirty miles from the Equator in the South Pacific.

They have been called guineapigs. But, as one of them pointed out to me, if you're a guineapig at least you get good medical attention so they can see what's happened to you. These servicemen got no subsequent medical attention to see what difference, if any, the nuclear tests had made to them.

They were sent, they were used, they were released and they dropped from sight. A generation later, that official indifference is being challenged. The tests have brought consequences that cannot be ignored. Far too many of the nuclear veterans are dead before their time. Exactly how many? Who knows? Certainly the Ministry of Defence doesn't. But the research I have done points to a minimum figure of two hundred. That is an estimate of *excess* deaths, over and above the normal expectancy. They were men who died before the age of fifty-five – often long before – of cancer, in particular the blood or bone cancers associated with radiation, such as leukemia.

In addition, research indicates a figure numbering into thousands of men who are in constant need of medical treatment of some kind or other; while a substantial minority are gravely ill or disabled.

This is not a book about the horrors of nuclear war, or deterrence, or the morality of having the weapons at all. It is about what thirty years of official neglect can do. For thirty years, British governments of both political stripes have poured money into nuclear weapons and spent nothing on the special needs of the men who, in the Fifties, helped make these developments possible. And for thirty years, many of those men have suffered for their service, and suffered increasingly.

Before I wrote this book I went around the country and heard the experiences of a lot of veterans at first hand. Much of what they told me I have quoted: they were there, they should know. Memory can play odd tricks, and I didn't accept absolutely everything I heard. Nevertheless, one fact emerged that is beyond dispute. After the tests, these men were forgotten. Twenty thousand young men had been deliberately and many of them repeatedly made witnesses of nuclear explosions at a time when radiation medicine was in its infancy, and thereafter every British government down through the years repeated the same official formula ('Nobody was at risk') without taking the smallest step systematically to check its truth by examining the only evidence that matters: the health of the men.

There may be a case for defending the nuclear tests on the grounds that we didn't know any better at the time. But what has happened since – or rather what has *not* happened – is indefensible. It's the story of thirty years of violent neglect.

*   *   *

Until 1960, every man who was eighteen and British and medically fit had to do two years' military service. (It went up from eighteen months when the Korean War broke out.) At that time, National Servicemen made up the bulk of the armed forces, especially the Army. Some men deferred their call-up until they had been to university or finished their apprenticeship, by which time they were 22 or 23. This raised the average age, but not by much: most National Servicemen went in at 18 and came out at 20. To understand National Service you have to understand the 1950s.

Britain was still recovering from the Second World War. The great never-had-it-so-good sea change of the 1960s had not begun; what Britain was recovering towards was a kind of restoration of the 1930s. Television was still nowhere, the cinema everywhere. Foreign holidays were for the rich. Cars were a largely middle-class privilege. Ordinary people never 'ate out'. Rationing had ended only yesterday. The social structure was still pretty rigid. I remember in 1958 going to a wedding. I was wearing Moss Bros full fig and tails. I was in the refreshment room at Victoria Station, drinking a cup of tea, when a working man got up and offered me his seat. At first I thought he was taking the mickey (as we said in those days) but I soon saw that the offer was genuine: he felt it was improper that I, dressed as I was, should stand while he sat. It made him uncomfortable.

I took the seat he offered. The British were an obedient lot then. Schoolboys always said 'sir', sometimes more than once ("Sir, sir, it it true, sir, what Brown says, sir?"). The rule at my state school was that all staff, both male and female, must be called 'sir'. The fact that I saw nothing odd about this just goes to underline my unquestioning respect for authority, especially masculine authority.

Thus in one regard, joining the RAF was easy: I simply went on saying 'sir' in the same automatic way to a different authority. In another respect it was culture shock on the grand scale. Like virtually all my fellow-conscripts this was the first time I had left home, apart from Boy Scout camps, and none of us was prepared for the blank, stony indifference with which we were treated. It was worse than contempt. The first order I was given in the RAF was: "Fuck off." The tone was flat and empty; it didn't have the strength to be insulting. The order came from an old sweat of an LAC to whom I had handed my call-up papers. He said the same to everyone. I suppose he thought it was an appropriate way to move us to the next stage of the induction process, and he was probably right.

It probably did me no harm, as a cocky 19-year-old, to be cut down to size and knocked into shape. But what new shape was I being made to fit? It turned out to be an old-fashioned pattern. The RAF, in the 1950s, had barely realised that it was in the jet age. You just had to look at us. We wore ammunition boots whose toecaps were supposed to be bulled to a shine we could shave in. Our uniforms were ill-fitting and made of a hairy serge that lost its crease at the mention of rain. Of all the Services, the RAF should have valued technical excellence above everything else; yet often the greatest attention was given to duties that owed their existence to the Edwardian Army. I served at stations where the CO's Inspection mattered more than anything else. Every item of kit had to be laid out on one's bed in a precise pattern: spare socks exactly here, buttonstick exactly there, waterbottle exactly parallel with buttonstick, and so on. (Why did airmen have waterbottles? Nobody knew. It was just something else to keep clean.) One CO was fanatical about this precision. If an item displeased him by a millimetre it went out of the window. I knew some regulars who kept complete *duplicate* sets of kit, never worn, to be used solely for CO's Inspection. Each item of clothing was immaculately folded around cardboard stiffeners, ready to be laid out like playing cards. That particular trick seems to me an apt metaphor for the ritual irrelevance of RAF life. Once we were trained, our work often turned out to be non-work or even anti-work. The truth was that there were far too many National Servicemen with far too little to do: but of course this must not be admitted, and so we developed a kind of polished brainlessness to disguise the fact.

I think the turning point in my understanding of National Service came when a corporal ordered me to sweep the operations room floor. Ten minutes later, I was just about to get rid of my little heap of dust when he stopped me. "Don't do that," he muttered. "If they see you standing around doing nothing I'll have to find you another job. Try and keep sort of, you know, spreading it about." So for the next hour I distributed and redistributed that dust, while seriously pretending to accumulate it. That is what I mean by polished brainlessness. It makes you feel that you are irrelevant and that the Service is pointless. It does not encourage you to ask questions or expect information or to assume that what is going on makes sense.

10

If I had been sent to Christmas Island, or Maralinga, or Monte Bello (and I might have been sent; I was in the right age group) that would have been that. I would have gone without question and when I got there I would have done as I was told – and if I was told very little about why I was doing it, that would have come as no surprise. I was just an airman, just a National Serviceman. They had more of us than they knew what to do with.

*   *   *

There were many regulars among the men who served at Maralinga, Monte Bello or Christmas Island. (Some did two tours of duty or more.) All the senior NCOs and nearly all the officers were regulars.

Many of them had served in the Second World War. This coloured their attitude towards the sharing of information, especially with National Servicemen. They preserved the war-time lesson that secrecy, like Guinness, is good for you. The more, the better, in fact. Excessive secrecy on Christmas Island and elsewhere had much the same effect as excessive Guinness: it overheated the imagination. When I was researching this book I met several ex-servicemen who recalled rumours that were taken, at the time, to be hard fact. It was said, for instance, that the lagoon at Christmas Island became so badly contaminated with radioactivity that it was placed out of bounds for swimming. It was said that Fanning Island, about 200 miles north-west of Christmas Island, had been obliterated by a nuclear test. It was said that a hydrogen bomb which exploded high in the air created a tidal wave that hit Hawaii, 1300 miles away. It was said that a different hydrogen bomb had set off a rainstorm that flooded Christmas Island. None of these reports was true, but clearly they satisfied a need at the time.

Apart from the insatiable military appetite for secrecy, there are three possible reasons why the ordinary serviceman was told so little about the nuclear tests he was obliged to witness.

One is the general tension of the 1950s.

The Korean War was a mainly American affair, but British troops fought there too, and for a while it looked as if the conflict might brew up into a major East–West confrontation. Reservists were called up in large numbers. It was a curious period: neither war nor peace. A band of Second World War pilots, all recalled reservists, arrived at Exeter airfield, where I was státioned. They paraded each morning in unbuttoned battledress and carpet slippers, to the fury of the Station Warrant Officer. Then they spent the day flying Spitfires at very low level, sometimes alongside the Cornish Riviera Express, to the alarm or delight of its passengers. This was cheerfully cavalier (although at least one Spitfire crashed) but the sense of crisis that prompted it was threatening enough. Only recently, Russia had tried to starve West Berlin into surrender by closing the air corridor, and it had taken a massive airlift by the Western Allies to beat off that challenge. After Korea came the Hungarian uprising, suppressed by Russia, and at the same time Britain and France (in cahoots with Israel) were fighting Egypt for the Suez Canal and much else.

It was a jumpy decade. People tended to see warclouds gathering whenever they looked out of the window. Thus Britain's nuclear weapons tests were a military secret at a time when the Powers were often engaged in push-and-shove. The secrecy of the tests was part of their potency. Tell nobody, least of all your own men. Especially when they are National Servicemen who, after all, are not real soldiers (or sailors, or airmen). Reason two.

And the third and greatest reason why officers and NCOs shared so little information about the tests with their men is that most of the time they knew nothing themselves.

Even so, it is hard to understand why the military's PR with its troops on places like Christmas Island was so dreadful as to be non-existent. The thin official news sheets that were issued were okay if you like potted squadron histories; after that they were bumf. No British or American newspaper or magazine reached the island unless a friend or relative sent it. No radio, except for a couple of privately owned shortwave sets. For most men, no official briefings before the tests, or afterwards; just an order to parade, and perhaps an announcement of success. The whole set-up was Soviet in its isolation. Christmas Island was a strange place. Don't take my word for it. Read on.

WITNESSES

We just weren't told anything. We didn't know anything at all, we were just told that we had to parade at four o'clock in the morning, and we were just marched a mile down the road from main camp towards the port camp, and we just sat beside the road. They didn't tell us anything that was going to happen. You know, we just sort of sat there and hoped it wouldn't be too bad. But the first test, you know, was a complete shock to all of us.

*   *   *

Just had your ordinary shirt on, bush hat, and we put a sweat-rag tied around our eyes and put our dark glasses on, and just put our hands over our eyes, sat down on the side of the road, and just sort of gazed in the distance, I suppose, with your back to where the explosion's going to be. And then when the Canberras came over the third time the commentator said 'This is a real live run'.

*   *   *

And then they said: 'Bombs gone.' And then of course you had a 30-to-1 countdown, thinking about this thing coming down towards you.

*   *   *

You could *see* the plane, and you could *see* this thing drop, and everybody had to turn round and hold the heels of their hands into their eyes; well I remember then, thinking that that was it, the time had come, because when that thing went off . . .

*   *   *

15

With our eyes closed in accordance with instructions, we were told we'd be blind if we didn't; with our sunglasses on; with our hands over our eyes.

*   *   *

And when he said three, two, one, zero, there was this blinding flash and we could all see straight through our hands, and you could see all the veins and all the bones and everything in your hands.

*   *   *

After the flash the most frightening part, in my estimation, was the heat. Because the heat built up to a crescendo.

*   *   *

Hot. Really warm. I'm a blacksmith. I was a blacksmith on the island. I was used to working up in the 80s . . . That didn't bother me one little bit, I work in the 80s, 90s! Shit, when that bomb went off – it was murder there. It was murder! That hurt me. It really hurt me.

*   *   *

I saw the flash, like a flashbulb set off right before my eyes. In the same instant I felt the heat through my shirt just as though someone had passed a blowlamp over my back.

*   *   *

Then there was a further count-up of 20 seconds. They said, 'Right, you can turn round and you can face the bomb.' We turned round and we faced the bomb. It was as though the world had suddenly developed two suns.

*   *   *

It was like a red sun, and it was just racing up, rather like a firework, these red fireworks that come out, and they explode into stars, well this didn't explode, it just raced upwards, and then the sea started to rise, to meet it. And then it all cascaded out into a big mushroom cloud.

*   *   *

I was in the REs myself and I knew what a blast was like, say from a TNT slab, you see. And it's similar to one of them going off about ten yards away. Just, didn't hurt you. Just pushed you forward. Like a blast. And that was the effect I had.

*   *   *

Stood there looking up, all of us, and amazed by it. And I remember the island was always surrounded by cloud but there was no cloud on the island itself. And I remember the clouds moving away from the centre. I can remember saying, 'That must be the shock wave.' And I'd hardly uttered the words and it hit us.

*   *   *

And there were blokes being thrown everywhere.

*   *   *

It was a gi-normous, I can only describe it as a metallic clang, I don't know, a million times bigger than you ever hear in a thunderstorm. And then there were several other minor clangs. And then a lot of rumbling.

*   *   *

That first mushroom cloud, watching it rise and watching these strange interlacing . . . like lampshades, one on top of the other, as the cloud went up, the column grew and the cloud went higher and higher.

*   *   *

There was two atomic bombs, but we just continued to work while they went off – we just got told they was goin' off and . . . What was an atomic bomb, it was only 20,000 tons, and

17

comparing it with a hydrogen bomb it was like a squib, somebody exploding a squib, that was all.

* * *

MONTE BELLO, 1952

Nobody said nothing about it; all we knew was that we was going abroad. But *where*, nobody knew, nobody didn't have any clues. We just sailed on, and sailed on . . . until you reached Australia. And then like somebody had a little bit of a guess then, and by all accounts the papers got hold of it . . . He was in the army, with us. I don't think he *meant* to give it away, you know what I mean? It was just somebody got it out of him. And he was court martialled for it. Oh yes, we was there at court martial. It was on deck. It was on deck in front of us. And that was the last I seen the bloke.

DOUGLAS ATWILL

A regular in the Royal Engineers when he sailed to Australia in 1952, Douglas Atwill witnessed one nuclear test. He suffers from what he describes as 'a slow crumbling away of his spine', plus muscle failure. He has been unable to work for the last five years (that is, since he was 48). His son, born soon after his return, suffers from similar muscular difficulties as well as swollen legs and large bumps on his body. Mr Atwill's other children are in good health.

* * *

There was a bit of a discussion on the way down, when we went down, but . . . the impression I got, it was like any bomb – once it had gone bang and all the muck had gone, you were all right.

WALTER THOMPSON

18

Walter Thompson was 22 when he went to Monte Bello with the Royal Navy. He witnessed one nuclear test. A year later he developed severe skin trouble (hands splitting and bursting open). This condition persisted when he left the navy. Eventually it became so severe that he was unable to work. (He was a self-employed dairyman.) Despite consulting many leading dermatologists he cannot find the cause of this complaint.

* * *

It was volcanic rock. Mostly. And sand. But a wonderful place for fishing. It was a bit boring, really. Because we went for seven months, and never saw a house, or a motorcar, or a woman even, for seven months. Very routine. We went to a couple of lectures from this RAF doctor which told us it would be quite safe, that we would be allowed so many milliroentgens of radioactivity – I forget the exact figure now, but it would be within the safety limits. But no one knew what sort of results they'd be, because it was the first British test.

JOHN TRIVETT

Aged 22 when he sailed to Monte Bello in HMS Tracker, a converted tank landing craft, John Trivett witnessed one nuclear test. His health is satisfactory.

* * *

When you're doing shelters, and Anderson shelters, and, you know, putting up cameras, you know there's something fishy going on, you know. Nobody ever come up to tell you that it was atomic bomb. Although you heard Dr Penney was on board the ship, and you had a good guess then; you knew that something was going on. Well I should say . . . when they came clean was the time when they had you on deck to get away from the bomb, to witness the bomb. I think that was the only time you ever *knew*, really, that it was an atomic bomb.

ATWILL

It was exploded in a river-class frigate, HMS *Plym*, which was 1,500 tons, and it just . . . well it just . . . vapourised.

ALBERT CLARK

Albert Clark was 29 when he went to Monte Bello as ship's butcher on board HMS Campania, *the flagship. He witnessed one nuclear test. After leaving the navy he suffered two nervous breakdowns. His physical health is satisfactory. His youngest son, born after Mr Clark's return, had to have all his milk teeth extracted when they turned black.*

* * *

There was five LCMs. Our job was the ferrying of all these scientists and things. Well, one of the LCMs was waiting on the beach to pick up the scientists who triggered this device. I'm not going to say how long they were given but they weren't given all that much time because they actually ran onto the beach, they ran onto the landingcraft, and the landingcraft was still inside the lagoon when the explosion took place. Between two and three miles away. No more than three.

FRANK GRAY

Frank Gray was 22 when he went to Monte Bello as a regular in the Royal Marines. He has suffered a range of serious complaints – in particular, granulation, a defect of the eyes that causes a 'cracked mirror' effect; nodules on the intestines; and severely swollen hands. One son and one daughter, born since his return, are tall and grossly overweight; the other son is abnormally thin and has virtually no hair. Of five grandchildren, one is so hyperactive as to need sedation; another is extremely undersized; and a third has a deformed nose – the nose is almost non-existent.

* * *

Dr Penney and them was up on deck, and then you got told that the bomb would be going off, and would we all face the other way. Which you did, really. And then he'd count down from ten to zero, and he'd say 'Now, when I say zero, give it a minute and then you can turn round and look at it.' So we said, well all right.

ATWILL

*   *   *

We got the reflection of the flash through the superstructure and off the flightdeck. And then, when the flash went – it lasted, hung for a few seconds – then we turned around and saw the cloud rising up, big white molten ball. Then we got the blast several . . . well, minutes later.

THOMPSON

*   *   *

You know, we couldn't understand why we had to stand with our backs to the thing. You had an element of lightheartedness and some people not bother, others would take it very seriously. I can recall just feeling, well this is a bit of a waste of time – what was the point of standing on deck and looking round at the thing *after* it had exploded?

IAN MCKENZIE

> *Ian McKenzie was 21 when he went to Monte Bello as an AB with the Royal Navy. He witnessed one nuclear test. He has a small patch of skin cancer on his chest, and has suffered periods of depression; otherwise his health is satisfactory.*

*   *   *

It didn't go like a mushroom like you see on the films. It was more like a Z shape. It started drifting one way, then the other, then back again.

GRAY

*   *   *

21

When the actual bomb went off we could see the cloud breaking back in the centre. It was supposed to go out to sea but it broke back in the centre and you could see the fall, like you would a storm, the rain coming from a storm, going back right across the islands, where it wasn't supposed to be.

THOMPSON

*   *   *

We were behind the islands, the highest ones I'd say were about 30 foot. We were told it was going to happen, but we didn't have a countdown for certain it was going to go off. We weren't warned of the actual minute that it was going up. So it came as rather a surprise. I was, actually I was trying to brew some tea, and the blast blew the primus over, so I still haven't got that cup of tea yet.

GRAY

*   *   *

I took parties of men ashore that did have the protective clothing. They used to come back in the evening, strip off all this clothing. It was put into 40-gallon drums with cement, to be ditched later. They'd go for showers and things. If they went ashore the next day they were given new clothing again. I think they wore gas masks. I don't recall being checked myself. The men we took ashore were not experienced in radiation: it was stokers, and able seamen; they were just picked out as shore landing party. Just picked at random. [Their job] was to plot safe areas, with these dosimeters. Geiger counter, I think they called it.

TRIVETT

*   *   *

About four days later, I went back in, in the boat and we went into the area, looking to see if we could find anything of the boat itself, the *Plym*. We went in over the actual spot, right over the spot. Right in the spot. We were actually looking in the water. Looking to see if there was anything left, and I can remember going back on the *Campania* and telling the boys that come off the *Plym*, 'No, there's nothing there, not a bloody bit of it left anywhere.'

THOMPSON

*   *   *

We made water from the sea water. All the time. And as far as I know, we never stopped making water. And although the bomb was exploded on the waterline, or below the waterline, it must have been very contaminated; and distilling water doesn't take radiation out; and so we were still drinking that water.

CLARK

*   *   *

And there was hundreds of men going in there, working in there, afterwards, for weeks afterwards. And I learnt since that they recovered the moorings. Recovered some of the moorings off the *Plym* and they was so contaminated that they had to take them out in deep water and dump them, they couldn't keep them on the ship.

THOMPSON

*   *   *

There was an incident just after the blast. We were in one of the lagoons – we called it a lagoon, because there were various inlets between the islands, something like the Norwegian fiords, you know? – and one night there was an alert, because they had fixed a geiger counter to an engine condenser, which takes seawater for cooling the steam, which has to be used again; and this geiger counter gave a rather high reading. And we raised full steam to make a quick manoeuvre. I remember that incident. About 2 a.m. one morning. There was a bit of a panic, to get the ship moving.

TRIVETT

None of the scientists or anything wore any protective clothing, that I knew. Or saw. And I was taking them all in, all the
prominent ones, Dr Butterworth, Dr Penney. Everyone was in
their shorts. Dr Penney used to run around with shorts and a
straw hat on. There was no protective clothing. None whatsoever. We had a badge they told us to pin on ourselves. It was
like a plastic thing with a square bit of lead or whatever it was
in there. And it was supposed to turn red if you got radioactive,
well, half of us didn't bother to put the bloody things on in the
morning, you know. You used to forget about them. You
never bothered. I never heard anyone say anything about
them. That was all we had. There was no . . . When we went in,
after that time, there was no one with us monitoring or
anything, we were just a boat's crew and we went in.

THOMPSON

* * *

It was a lovely sight, mind, I'm not saying it wasn't, but . . . I
don't want to see another bomb. I wouldn't see another one.

ATWILL

* * *

It was just like a great big holiday really. You know, we treated
it as a great big skylark.

THOMPSON

* * *

MONTE BELLO, 1956

What used to be the tank deck had been lopped off and turned
into a refrigerated hold. There was supposed to be four sets of
refrigeration gear, so if one fell over the panic bell would go

and the next one took over, because inside there was the TNT RDX, which was the outer casing. This had been specially machined so that it formed round the actual ... what's it called? ... we'll say anyway, plutonium core. And it was all bolted up and it *had* to keep its shape. If it lost its shape you would get a fine jet of plutonium come out, and *our* troubles would be over, and nobody would be able to go there for about 700 years.

RON BRITTAIN

Ron Brittain was 28 when he went to Monte Bello as a leading seaman/diver. He witnessed two nuclear tests. He suffers 'a lot' from migraine and depression, perhaps better described as a state of total emotional indifference.

*   *   *

The special compartments were under armed guard up to the point of conducting the tests. Outside was the Royal Marine on guard, even at sea, in the middle of the Indian Ocean, there he stood with his rifle and bayonet.

REG COLLIER

Reg Collier was 27 when he went to Monte Bello as a petty officer. He witnessed two nuclear tests. Apart from a persistent rash and redness of the skin his health has been satisfactory. His daughter was born soon after his return to the UK; she is mentally handicapped.

*   *   *

We had a ship's programme laid down for us, eventually ending at the Monte Bello islands, and we knew that we were going to witness a test out there, because we were given instruction in NBCD, as we called it, which is ... nuclear warfare. So we saw the films from Hiroshima and Nagasaki – which at that time were not on release to the general public – and we were given basic details about the effects of radiation, etc. etc. But very basic. It was a huge adventure. At eighteen years of age . . . really we were innocents abroad at that particular time. We weren't worried about radiation or the longterm effects of radiation because such a subject hadn't ever come up. It was something totally new. To us, it was just an adventure.

ROBERT MALCOMSON

Robert Malcomson was 18 in 1956, a telegraphist on the destroyer HMS Diana. *He was later commissioned and served in all 17 years in the Navy.*

*   *   *

We had film badges all the time, and they were most strict, the officers, that you wore the film badge *all* the time. And you wore that on your No. 8 shirt ['No. 8' was regular everyday working uniform], and I think periodically, maybe every month, it was taken away.

GEOFF MAUGHAN

Geoff Maughan was 23 when he went to Monte Bello as a leading electrician's mate. He witnessed four nuclear tests (including two at Christmas Island). At the age of 46 he suddenly collapsed. The cause was diagnosed as an underactive thyroid gland. With treatment he has made a full recovery.

*   *   *

Of course you'd been building up to this big thing . . . We'd been hectically hard at work – probably some of the hardest work in my life – in terrible conditions of heat; and *Narvik* had no air conditioning, and in the met office just below the upper deck it got up to 140 Fahrenheit. We worked just in shorts and sandals, sometimes without sandals, sometimes without shorts. We just sat in the met office, plotting charts, and we had blotting paper on the met charts, and we beavered away – day and night, of course, round the clock . . . We had blotting paper to soak up the sweat as we plotted the charts.

COLLIER

*   *   *

We all wore badges during the test, because *Diana*'s purpose in that test was to steam through the fallout. (Unfortunately, the first explosion, we were supposed to go through the fallout at that particular time, but the meteorological people made a slight mess of it and we missed the fallout. We were in the wrong position. So we had to go and do it once again.) We were more or less a guinea-pig ship to test what would happen to a warship under those conditions. It was the first time it had been done, and they set up a pre-wetting system, which is hoses to sprinkle water over the ship, which was meant to wash away the radiation as the dust fell on board. And we were taken down to shelter stations, beneath the waterline, for 13 hours. The ship was sealed up into an airtight citadel and the prewetting sprinkler system was switched on. We were closed up at shelter stations and spent 13 hours going through this cloud. Those on watch, the engineering branch, had a pretty tough time because they had to wear a type of spacesuit with their own breathing apparatus, and the engineroom of course was closed down, so it was extremely hot for those people. And quite a lot of them came back to the mess afterwards with bad burns on their shoulders etc. because of the heat of the air they were actually breathing.

Unfortunately the system of prewetting didn't quite work the way they hoped it would and a large part of the ship was contaminated. The engineroom intakes were badly contaminated, a lot of the deck plating, some of the gun-mountings . . . So the Australian government wouldn't let us back in, and we had to steam to the naval dockyard in Singapore, where we were decontaminated, a lot of plates were removed, by cutting; and then we were allowed to go loose again. We knew that we had taken more radiation than they thought was possible. They thought it would be washed away, but it wasn't. And the parts of the ship that were badly contaminated were actually roped off, and none of the crew was allowed to go near it. We had scientists on board, and there was quite a lot of running to and fro with geiger counters etc.

MALCOMSON

We were there in '56; in 1952 HMS *Plym* – the first British atomic test – had been vaporised, not so far from where we dropped anchor. But obviously a surface burst of a vessel of 1,500 tons was vaporised, a very dirty blast, and there was a lot of radioactive fallout. Although it was four years previous, the decay rate of radioactivity is slow enough that there must have been some pretty hot spots there, even four years later. And the ship being in the sea, my concern is the fact that there was a great proliferation of tropical fish, we used to catch it over the side and cook it in the galley and so forth. Even if you weren't near to the tests at the time of the explosion, people eating the fish, living ashore, distilling the water from seawater – this was also the case after our *first* test, they were still living ashore there, and distilling their seawater through the purification plant – that sort of thing is of concern to me, because people could have accumulated small doses of contamination without even knowing it.

COLLIER

*   *   *

In 1974 I had trouble reading, and I thought, 'Well, I'm getting a little old, perhaps it's time I had glasses'. And I went to see an optician, and he started to test my eyes and couldn't complete the test, because he said, 'There's a film of blood across your eyes, you'd better go to Southampton General Hospital, and have it checked right away.' So I went across to the eye hospital, and they couldn't figure it out, and quite a lot of tests took place over the next three weeks to find out what the problem was, and the initial diagnosis in actual fact was psittacosis, which is a parrot's disease and a tropical disease. And so – it was quite funny, really – they went to my home, the local council people dressed in white spacesuits with tongs, took the budgie and his cage away, and put him to sleep; and the poor little devil was innocent all the time. So eventually they came up with my complaint, which is polycythaemia;

28

which is a blood disorder. That means that my marrow makes too many red blood cells.

In those days, in the early Seventies, every time I had a drink, my eyes became bright red, and the blood was actually coming through in my nose, and my lips . . . When they X-rayed me in the hospital, my lungs were completely shadowed and they were just filled with blood. And within a 3-day period, when they discovered what it actually was, they took away just over six pints of blood, in three days. It had got to such a stage it was just very, very thick. And . . . had that optician not sent me to the General Hospital I wouldn't be here today.

That was eleven years ago, and since then every six weeks I go to Southampton General Hospital, where they take just over a pint of blood away, to control it. Then my system's fine. It's the only thing that they can do for it, in actual fact. The red cells just build up and build up and if they didn't take the blood away, of course I would just collapse. Had I been older, they can inject a radioactive isotope into the marrow, which will dampen down the production of red cells; but they only do that in extreme cases. I've managed to carry on eleven years now with this, and lead a normal, active life. I was told at one period that the length was ten years, and then you either got a reversal where you became anaemic, or you had slight problems, you know. Not buying any long-playing records, and things like this. But I've carried on eleven years and still feel very fit and well.

I know there's a lot of criticism of the government etc. . . I don't criticise, because I was doing a job that I was paid for. I loved the Royal Navy, I had a marvellous 17 years. I honestly don't think they themselves knew what they were talking about when it comes to the longterm effects of radiation. As far as compensation for those who have suffered – and there are quite a number of them, as you know – I would want nothing for myself, but I do think that the wives and families of serving members who have died from leukemia, from cancer, from various other blood disorders, and there are a lot of them, I think they should be helped. I think really if we asked members of the government who are opposing this to go on board a warship, knowing what they do nowadays, and steam through a fallout cloud from a nuclear explosion, I wonder how many would be willing to do it. Then we were innocents, now we're not quite.

MALCOMSON

*   *   *

CHRISTMAS ISLAND

Just one big sandpile with coconut trees.

KEN TAYLOR

Ken Taylor was 21 when he went to Christmas Island as a cook with the Royal Navy. He witnessed seven nuclear tests. At 24 he began to suffer persistent vomiting and sickness. From the age of 26 he has been treated for multiple stomach ulcers. In 1983, when he was 47, cataracts were diagnosed in both eyes. He has had successful operations for these.

*   *   *

We flew in I think it was on an American Airlines' Stratocruiser, and we could go up and look round the cabin, the flightdeck. And I was up there virtually when we sighted Christmas Island, and the pilot said, 'There you are, fellas, there's your home for the next so-many months.' And it was a tiny little strip of sand on the horizon, and I thought, well, we've come something like twelve hundred and fifty miles from Honolulu; and if he'd have deviated a fraction of a degree, we'd have missed it and gone on to the Antarctic, I'm sure. It looked so diminutive, in all this ocean . . .

JOHN LYCETT

30

John Lycett was 23 when he went to Christmas Island as a National Serviceman in an RAF Balloon Unit. He witnessed four nuclear tests. His health has been satisfactory. His daughter was born after his return to Britain; her milk teeth were without enamel. The second set was normal.

*   *   *

When we arrived at Christmas Island in late January 1958 – it took us almost a month to get there – it was a beautiful morning, you could see the little island and the coral reef and the tide coming in and breaking against the reef, it was a lovely . . . it was one of these picture islands that you see, tropical island, very beautiful at six o'clock in the morning.

KEN MCGINLEY

Ken McGinley was 23 when he went to Christmas Island with the Royal Engineers. He witnessed five nuclear tests. Since his return he has suffered a range of debilitating complaints: duodenal ulcer, malfunctioning kidney, rapid dental decay, persistent rash, swollen legs and hands.

*   *   *

It was three in the morning and when they opened the door to the plane when we arrived there, this blast of hot air came in like a furnace, and we stepped outside and the stench from rotting vegetation nearly knocked you down. You got used to it after about two days, and you didn't notice it after that. But the first impression I got was 'Oh God – what have we come to?' You know: surely this isn't going to be where we'll be living for the next six months? It was sheer horror to start with.

TOM CHARMAN

Tom Charman was 25 when he went to Christmas Island as a Signals corporal. He witnessed one nuclear test. He and his children are in satisfactory health.

31

It was clean-looking, very sunny, white beaches, blue lagoons
– quite pleasant to look at, really. I wouldn't say it was ideal
but it was interesting. At 23 it would be, wouldn't it?

ARCHIE ROSS

*Archie Ross was 23 when he went to Christmas
Island as an RAF corporal instrument fitter. He
witnessed six nuclear tests. 18 months after he
returned, his first child was born with a gross deformity of the right arm and chest. He suffers from a
rare eye complaint.*

*   *   *

I mean, it's flat; it's featureless; there's nothing to impress.

CHARMAN

*   *   *

Wonderful, it were . . . Oh, beautiful place. I mean, the wild
life sort of thing, birds, fish, view of the sea, underwater, things
like that, were terrific. The most distinct thing I remember is
the sea was as clear as could be. You could see the bottom at
200 foot. And really pick things out, y'know, 200 foot deep. I
remember I lost a watch. I was painting the ship's side one day
and I dropped a watch over the side. And I could literally see it
go down and down and down and down, until it settled on the
bottom. And it was amazing, y'know, the clarity of the water.
It was . . . unbelievable.

WALLY JACKSON

*Wally Jackson was 19 when he went to Christmas
Island on HMS* Messina. *He witnessed three nuclear
tests at Malden Island. He has suffered persistent
rashes on his feet and legs. His four children are
healthy; one stillborn child was deformed.*

*   *   *

I remember very definitely the surprise I got to see all the coconut palms in dead straight rows. It struck me as most odd.

JOHN McLENNAN

John McLennan was 22 when he went to Christmas Island as a National Serviceman in the Royal Engineers. He witnessed one nuclear test. Soon after his return to Britain he developed leukopenia (an abnormal reduction of white blood cells in the blood) and after a series of illnesses he nearly died of meningitis. His health is now satisfactory.

*　　*　　*

But you got used to it after two or three days, and you accepted it for what it was: it was just a pile of coral and a few plants and a few birds, and that was it – there just *wasn't* anything else, much. There's a bush which was called a tie bush, which is totally useless, cos you can't burn it, you can't eat it, you can't use the fronds for anything, it didn't have fruit. And that grew all round the main camp. And it's absolutely a useless thing, but it rots and it smells horrible.

CHARMAN

*　　*　　*

I mean ... if you can visualise an army camp, which is normally a pretty desolate sort of place surrounded by walls, well if you can imagine walls being a few hundred miles of sea ... I mean, Hawaii – the only place of any size – was thirteen hundred miles away ... You did feel pretty cut-off. There was certainly very little there to do, other than the job in hand. And I think three thousand men on their own is not really the ideal arrangement.

McLENNAN

*　　*　　*

'Twas absolutely tremendous. We had one of the best twelve months I've ever had in my life as a boy. I had some of the best companions I've ever met, and I still think about it. It was one big holiday, bar working; and we worked very hard there, they paced us out something terrific, we were working twelve hours a day there. We were swimming in the lagoons every weekend . . . Every weekend we always got our compo rations and went to the Naafi and picked our beer up and went off to the lagoons. We cooked on the lagoon side, we swam continuously in the lagoons . . .

GARY COLLINS

Gary Collins was 21 when he went to Christmas Island with the Royal Engineers. He witnessed five nuclear tests. Since then he has suffered periodically from a severe rash on his face, arms and scalp.

*   *   *

We got to Christmas Island, we slept on the beach, we slept on the beach for a week and we brought the machinery ashore and built a port on Christmas Island, there was a port there, and roughly squared the port up, and we cut a road through which was to base camp was about something like I dunno nine, twelve mile long up through the coconut plantation, and the air strip was to be made up there, and basically we got the air strip roughly cut out.

BRIAN GILLMAN

Brian Gillman was 18 when he went to Christmas Island with the Royal Engineers. He witnessed five nuclear tests. Four years after his return, he developed a severe and persistent rash and multiple lumps on his body; despite prolonged treatment, both these conditions are unexplained. 1967 his son was born with grossly deformed feet: the feet were reversed, with the toes pointing backwards. Five years of intensive treatment corrected this.

*   *   *

Basically there was the main camp, there was the naval side and there was the airfield. There were no roads at the time –

there were just typical hard-packed sand roads – but the British Army in the next three months completed 25 miles of road. Worked extremely hard; I've never seen people work harder in my bloody life out there . . . We would go to work at seven o'clock in the morning, and they'd be working on the roads, and we'd return again at two o'clock in the afternoon and they'd still be working on the roads, until five o'clock at night. This is the British army, the Royal Engineers. I would like to point out they were all five feet tall, but most of them were five foot bloody wide!

Ross

*　　*　　*

We worked from dawn to dusk, had no lights in our tents, no recreation facilities, no showers or baths, so when we finished work, we ate, cleaned ourselves as best we could and went to bed. It was about three months before we had our first day off.

John Barnes

> *John Barnes, an RAF corporal wireless fitter, was in the landing party on Christmas Island 'right at the beginning of the operation'.*

*　　*　　*

We certainly did work hard, we were on the go all day six days a week. We had the Sunday off, I remember, and I remember when Christmastime came we were told that we were going to have Christmas Day and Boxing Day off. And this we were obviously rather pleased to hear. And we were told we were going to work the Sunday before and the Sunday after to make up for it, which really dampened our Christmas spirit quite considerably.

McLennan

*　　*　　*

The advance party of 400 Army and some 40 RAF personnel arrived on Christmas Island on the troopship *Devonshire*

35

which we boarded at Fiji. Our equipment was on board a tank landing craft, HMS *Narvik*, which was awaiting us. I cannot speak for the troops but none of the RAF had any past experience of stevedoring so it was a real eye-opener when we were told our tents, bedding and food were on the *Narvik* and if we wanted it we had best fetch it. It then transpired that the stores 'we' required had been loaded first so were at the bottom rear of the LCT and the Government's 'clutter' stood between us and it. Some smart-ass had his head screwed on!

My most vivid recollection is wading ashore chest-deep in water with a 5-gallon jerrycan of fuel, petrol, diesel, oil, etc., balanced on a raw and sunburnt shoulder. God there were thousands of those damn things.

BARNES

* * *

We arrived straight from England, it was a tremendous shock, the change in temperature, and very high humidities – the humidities I remember in particular, because I soon found I couldn't wear my glasses, although I'm very shortsighted. Because the water was constantly dripping off one's eyebrows, – I realised what eyebrows are for but they just weren't good enough – and dripping onto the lenses of one's glasses. And I just got so fed up with not being able to see through them I didn't wear them.

McLENNAN

* * *

People did have the choice: those who didn't like the sun could work through the night. It was non-stop, 24 hours around the clock. Rigged up a stonecrusher that crushed up the coral in different sections . . . A fleet of tipper lorries – thirty, maybe more, feeding from the stonecrusher to the cement mixer, and this massive gigantic great cement mixer, fed by a huge great skip with cement going into it non-stop . . . And this thing pushed out the cement, and then they had a fleet of dumpers, queuing up! Zooming it away! And then they had another workforce of guys with ... putting down shuttering, and laying it all ... Realise, it was going on 24 hours round the clock! With the stonecrusher to the cement mixer to the dumper to the guys laying the concrete – the organisation was great.

GILLMAN

*   *   *

No bull, no parades. None whatsoever on the island. We were a proper working regiment, we were treated purely as workmen. I should think 80% of the men that were with me were National Servicemen, they were all ex-craftsmen because we were all 21 when we joined up, not the average age of 18 ... And we all had served our time, every man was a craftsman in my squadron. And I think we were picked for that one reason. Cheap labour, I suppose, in a way. We were only getting about £7 or £8. We got £2 overseas allowance. And we worked damn hard.

COLLINS

*   *   *

Rough. Bloody rough. I found it rough. For a start ... Not because we was living in tents. I was used to that, because I was in the Boys Brigade and Scouts and everything else, I was used to that. But you know, there was nothing there. You couldn't do nothing, just work. Go and have a few bevvies and then back to bed and get on with the work again. But ... after a time we got used to it. Well we had to, really, I suppose.

A good Naafi. No Naafi girls, no. There was two WVS women; they must have been about 90 at the time, I should think. But every day they looked marvellous. Always made you welcome. Yeah. I say they were 90 years old – they were 25 years older than what we were, you see, you know. But a nice pair of women.

BRIAN TATE

37

Brian Tate, a regular in the Royal Engineers, was on Christmas Island for almost all of 1958, building the officers' mess and billets.

MALDEN ISLAND

Strictly speaking, the first three explosions in the Christmas Island series didn't take place at Christmas Island; they happened at Malden Island, a very small atoll 480 miles to the south. Brian Gillman was one of 49 men of the Royal Engineers who went there early in 1957 to prepare for the blasts.

Malden Island was very . . . oh, nobody lived there at all, just two or three trees. It was an atoll. Five miles around, water in the centre. And the boffins told us that obviously it grew over the years of coral and the bomb went off they even anticipated that the stem would break and possibly the atoll would slip off its stem (which never did happen). Basically we cut a small airstrip to get a tiny, well an old Dakota so they could get in there. Grub was dropped every ten days, dehydrated grub. We could either work through the day or through the night, you had the choice. You just was working, you wasn't sort of doing parades, you wasn't in the Army, you just . . . didn't shave very much, in other words you was just working-force. They had things to do: we had to dig things and bury things and machinery slowly came out there which we dug and buried, these fantastic great holes and . . . The cargo boats came out there, such as the *Wave Prince* and the *Ben Wyvis* and a few other of that, and we unloaded them out at sea, outside the coral reef, on . . . um . . . *platforms*, they was, floating platforms

38

. . . Some gear we lost, others we got ashore, I mean I can remember a brand new D8 bulldozer come over the side on the platform and it capsized and *sunk*, and that was the end of *that*.

GILLMAN

*　　*　　*

One way of getting men and equipment to and from Malden Island was in a Duck, the name given to a 7-ton six-wheeled amphibious vehicle.

Well when you came in with a Duck, you . . . It was a bit like surfing, you had to pick your wave and you couldn't hesitate, you chose your wave and whichever one you chose, and when it came you give it full revs. In you went, and you *surfed* in on that wave, and you pulled the lever to inflate the wheels at the same time, hit the shelf, the water gripped and up you went. And it was great! *But* . . . if you was buggered and you hit the shelf and you didn't go up with the wave, the next one came on your arse-end and tipped you up, you see. So it was all a case of judgement, luck, everything going all right – in on the surf, pull the lever, inflate the wheels, full revs with your wheels, full revs behind on your prop, hit the shelf, up the beach and you'd got away with it.

GILLMAN

*　　*　　*

I was given the task of packing up a small portable radio station and radio beacon and packed off to Malden Island (the target). One RAF corporal (self), 40 Royal Engineers and six met men now found ourselves the most unwelcome passengers on another LCT, HMS *Messina*. We dragged off down to Malden Island and on arrival the 47 of us set to and unloaded her with a speed no Port Authority would believe. Ship standing off the shore, bow doors open, ramp down, LCM (two of which we brought with us) LCM races for the ramp, rides up into the LCT, keeps engine on full throttle, step out of bow door, pass up chain to crewman of LCM, he hooks on, cut engines, LCM slides back, chains 'twang' taut, lower LCM ramp and load, reverse process, race for shore and is unloaded. Build new camp, build runway, set up radio station and five weeks later I am relieved.

BARNES

*   *   *

We had a guy there on the beach, he was called Lieutenant Jasper Baker, Royal Marines – ex-Marine wrestling and boxing champion. He was a great guy – but he only told you once. He told you *once*, very polite man, very well-spoken. He told you *once*. And even if you said, 'Sorry, sir? Pardon?', he'd literally give you a righthander. True. We knew this to be facts.

GILLMAN

*   *   *

The sappers usually unloaded cargo ships onto landing-craft. When one of these craft hit the beach and the drawbridge came down it was essential to make fast quickly, before it swung round and got sand up the intake pipe.

This particular day . . . Hit the beach, and a newcomer was on board, I suppose he was in the Marines, or Navy, poor guy, and I chucked the rope to him, he stood there, he didn't know what to do with it. I tried to shout to him, to tell him what to do. They made fast the other one, the LCM's swinging round, and this Jasper Baker, he climbed up this thing like a big spider. He *did*, he climbed up this like a big spider, and he got on there and he *hit* this poor guy *whoof!* A righthander, knocked him straight in the oggin. He was a 'eller, I tell you, this bloke Baker. A great guy! Like I can remember a Geordie falling over the side, couldn't swim, drowning! In went this bloomin' Jasper Baker, out he went like Garth, swam right . . . got hold, 'Come 'ere, you bugger,' he said. 'E was a great guy! Being all in together on the island, in close contact, you was all one big

40

team. There was no . . . You respected the captain, lieutenant, sergeant, but you was all working-force, you know?

*   *   *

Things started shaping up, and they said that, y'know, they're gonna do these tests. And then we had so many lectures what was going to happen, regards to . . . um . . . they didn't really know, expect blast and . . . winds hundred mile an hour, things like that.

GILLMAN

*   *   *

Before the first test, as a precaution against blast and heat, the sappers buried all their equipment – mounted cranes, bulldozers, scrapers – and all their personal belongings. The scientists and most of the sappers were taken off the island on Ducks the day before the explosion. Five men, including Gillman, stayed behind and worked all night, fuelling and switching on the machinery installed by the scientists. The explosion was scheduled for 1000 hrs. At 0900 they were picked up by a helicopter (which was two hours late) and flown to HMS Warrior, *an aircraft carrier. After a quick meal the five sappers were ordered to the flight deck, where they found the rest of their unit as well as large numbers of sailors, airmen and some Royal Marines. All those who could be spared from their duties below were on deck.*

The Tannoy's going away – 'Yeah, he's gone in, he's done a dummy run, it's all go, it's all systems go this time,' and we're all getting tensed, and I dunno, there was hosepipe on the deck, not being used, I picked it up, tied it round meself and said to me mate, 'Well, I ain't gonna go over the bloody side, at least I'm making fast,' anticipating that some . . . Because, on the flight deck there's no rails, there's just a flat top, there's nothing! You can't even put your knees on nothing. And anticipating, expecting wind hundred mile an hour, or blast, I mean . . . *Instinct* . . . And so to me, there we was, bomb gone,

41

countdown and . . . sitting there with our backs to the blast. Hosepipe wrapped round me. Hands over the goggles. And like everybody says, yes, fair enough, you could see the bone structure in the hands. This crack, rumbling like thunder. We turned round, still with the goggles on and looked, and I can remember – people got different versions, but I can remember a black bubble which I was told was the sun, and then this sort of deeply reddy fireball still erupting . . . and slowly that died, the colour died out . . . and the stem starts to grow up to the dome. And then finally we're told to clear the flight deck. No wind, no blast, I was a little bit disappointed, really.

GILLMAN

*   *   *

The first time they dropped the bomb at Malden Island, we came back from Malden Island the day after, and I can remember people at Christmas Island saying that they'd seen the flash and could tell us exactly what time this bomb went off, and bearing in mind that this is in bright sunlight at half-past ten in the morning in the tropics, and people 480 miles away had seen the flash . . .

JACKSON

I always remember the noise it made. If you can imagine standing under a bridge, with an express train going over the top, only going two or three hundred times louder – that's the sort of noise the first one made. And . . . well, in fact the second one was a very similar noise but a bit more compact and a bit louder. The third one: that went with a bang. That was a big bang.

JACKSON

*   *   *

I was on the *Messina*, just off Malden Island. The first time in fact there was only, I believe, three on the upper deck. We were the wheelhouse crew and the engineroom crew, and we sat on

42

the engineroom cowlings in a pair of white shorts, for all the number eights and anti-flash gear and that that they reckon everybody had, we didn't. I can remember three of us sat on the engineroom cowling, just outside the wheelhouse door, while this bomb went off, with nothing else other than that on.

The ship was battened down, everything was shut down, for at least six hours. I can remember going down – I was on the morning watch, well the forenoon, which is eight till twelve – and I can remember going down off watch at twelve o'clock to get lunch in the diningroom, and there was pools of sweat all over the floor in the diningroom, and in the messdeck, where blokes had been laid, because all the ventilator fans had been switched off, all the scuttles were closed, all the hatches, deck-doors, everything was all shut down. And these poor buggers had been laying on the benches, y'know. And the sweat had been *rolling* out of them. Absolutely pouring out of them. And I remember it was all over the floor, everywhere. Like walking in half-inch water. . . . Just . . . nothing but sweat! It was an amazing sight, really. And that was simply and purely because nobody seemed to be knowing what we should be doing. We hadn't had any instruction from *Narvik*, or what instruction we had had, somebody had got mixed up. And it turns out after that nobody was supposed to be downstairs, they was all supposed to be on the upper deck, watching this thing go off. And nobody actually *saw* it go off, other than those on the upper deck, and I was one of the three. And I remember that everybody else was sweating it out while I was – what I thought at that time – was enjoying myself, you know!

JACKSON

*   *   *

We laid off all night, and then in the morning we was all back on the island by ten o'clock . . . shovels out, digging out, because we'd buried 26-ton mounted cranes, the bulldozer, everything we owned, the scrapers . . . I mean, bloody great holes we dug to bury them all . . . Every bit of machinery we owned was buried. We had to get it all out. Get the canvas out, tents for the night time, things like getting the cookhouse rigged up and the toilets and things, and just getting straightened up in general . . .

GILLMAN

Two weeks later the sappers had to bury everything again, before the second test, and then dig it all up again. Another two weeks passed, and then they buried everything again, and after the third test they dug it all up again.

*   *   *

Ernest Cox was an Assistant Trials Planning Officer in the Atomic Weapons Research Establishment (AWRE). A helicopter took him from HMS Warrior *to Malden Island about fifteen hours after the explosion of the H-bomb.*

There were eight of us being taken. Before lift off I did ask if we had had clearance from Health Physics, the answer came back, yes it has been monitored. I thought then that has been damn quick. We were approaching the island, I didn't even have a film badge, and we hadn't a monitor between us. However I thought it must be clean. Soon after we landed at the old camp site, then some engineers from the army arrived. They immediately dug out some of the equipment from the dug-outs and Land-Rover which we had to use. However, after a while an Army Sergeant, my helper and myself took off up the island to retrieve some of my instruments, but before I did this I did ask a principal Scientific Officer if he had seen any of the Health Physics Team about it, and he said it was rather strange, no. . . . By late evening two showers had been erected so I went and had a good shower. Next day, back up the island again; in the evening I went for another shower which was very welcome. I had just taken my shorts off etc., when a chap came in with a monitor and he said let me run it over you. He did and to his amazement I had a reading of 3.80 Rs and another chap with me had a reading of 4.20 Rs so the Health Physics chap said what the hell could it have been yesterday – we would liked to have known. This was a contaminated area and we should have been issued with the protective clothing – we didn't see any, not even a film badge.

I worried no more about that, but a few days after, I had another worry. Two-thirds of my body was covered in blisters, so thick you couldn't put a pin between them. It was horrible and frightening. The Medical Officer on HMS *Warrior* just stared at me and said, 'Bloody hell, I've never seen anything like this before.' He thought it may be the water, then decided it couldn't be.

Ernest Cox was flown to Christmas Island for examination, tests and X-rays; eventually he was flown back to England. By then about half the blisters had vanished.

*   *   *

They never did clear 100%, and I never did have a medical on my return [to Aldermaston]. That surprised me. No-one seemed to be bothered. Everyone seemed more excited about the last explosion, which was a 5-megaton, the largest one ever . . . I could understand all of us being excited, but there were other things going on in the area of the explosion I was deeply concerned about . . .

The safety precautions, as far as I was concerned, the precautions were not strict. I wasn't spoken to once about safety, so I just got on with my work, not thinking of the dangers I could have been in.

Cox

*   *   *

We had these so-called film badges. All we had on was bush hats, shorts and boots, and we just pinned it onto our waist, onto our shorts. It was a thing about . . . oh . . . two inches long by an inch wide, metal case, with a little tiny strip open at the top on the front and a square at the bottom; and it was orange in colour. And we was *told*, we was definitely *told*, that if you pass anything radioactive, that will change to the colour of yellow. And if you did you would be flown back by the fastest means possible back to the UK. We was told by a captain in charge of us 49 Royal Engineers, who was informed and had lectures from the boffins. And so we sort of *believed* in these badges, if you like. We kept them with us. They say they was collected but I can assure you ours wasn't collected. (And also nobody's changed yellow.) In fact I brought mine home and gave it to Mother . . .

GILLMAN

*   *   *

Absolute wonder, that something so beautiful could be so devastating and so destructive. It's as simple as that. You see the shock-wave coming out from it, and . . . It's a terrific sight, beautiful. In the middle it varies from . . . oh . . . all sorts of colours . . . like fire-glow colours, y'know . . . right through the range, right through the spectrum. You have the red colour to an outside of *pure* white which even clouds in the sky don't seem to possess the same whiteness. And yet it's so devastating and so destroying.

JACKSON

*   *   *

Malden Island, the water supply was obviously nil. The [desalination] plant on the beach was a very tiny thing, and when you're really gasping for a drink, the first mouthful was all right, the second was a bit bitter, and the third was *'orrible*, you just couldn't drink the third one, you know? We'd got some beer ashore, canned beer, so we was drinking the canned beer. We used to bury it in the sand to keep it cold for the evening time, but then, time the tide had been washing around, you could never find half the cans, so I expect there's still thousands of cans buried there now . . .

GILLMAN

46

CHRISTMAS ISLAND AGAIN

We didn't have many fireworks out here, but I bet we had a bigger one than you did.

> *LAC Terry Hooper, writing to his parents on 10 November 1957*

*   *   *

We knew nothing, knew nothing at all. All we knew we was going abroad, and that was it. We didn't know nothing, where we was going or anywhere. We flew out there. I was National Service. I was 19 when I went out there. The day after we got out there we knew what we was out there for.

RAYMOND EDKINS

> *Raymond Edkins went to Christmas Island with the Royal Engineers. He witnessed one nuclear blast. Apart from a persistent rash and warty growths on the skin he is fit; but he has been sterile since his return to the UK.*

*   *   *

It was a big holiday to us, we were only young boys then. I was 21 . . . We were young boys, we never heard of H-bombs or A-tests in our lives.

COLLINS

*   *   *

We didn't know actually what we were going to do when we got there. And . . . in fact we didn't even know that they were going to be having hydrogen bomb tests at all, or the fact that we were ever going to be anywhere near them. We were told we were going to be the permanent maintenance squadron on the island.

JOHN IRVING

> *John Irving was 19 when he went to Christmas Island as a National Serviceman in the Royal*

Engineers. He witnessed two nuclear tests. At 36 he had a heart attack; at 41 he had a slight stroke. He recovered from both. In 1954, when he was 47, he developed a cataract in one eye.

* * *

When we went there it was only tents with the old-fashioned-type canvas beds with a very flimsy type steel structure on it. And we were given mosquito nets and two sheets and a blanket and a pillow and that was your lot. There was no type of furniture other than a bedside cabinet, beside your bed and I believe there was steel lockers that you hang your clothes on . . . But it was very, very primitive indeed, the surroundings.

McGINLEY

* * *

The food was plain, it was ordinary, it wasn't *that* bad, it was edible . . . We used to moan like mad about it but we always used to moan about the food wherever you went. It wasn't that bad – but it wasn't that good, either . . . The first morning we were there we got bacon and eggs and rhubarb and custard on the same plate, all in one dollop.

CHARMAN

* * *

The food on the island was out of this world. I mean, there wasn't an overseas base in the world that were fed like us.

COLLINS

* * *

The food was . . . not brilliant. But we did get some fresh fruit etc. that was flown in. I can remember green sausages, which I just couldn't stomach – presumably had been kept a bit on the long side. Certainly the army caterers didn't do the best they could with the food, by a long way. The eggs and suchlike would always be like rubber, and a rubbery fried egg is never

48

very nice. But then it was probably no different to the catering standards we had anyway, in the forces . . .

McLennan

* * *

I was walking past the cookhouse, one of the cooks had sides of beef hanging up and they were absolutely crawling with maggots. And he was throwing petrol over them and he set them alight. And I said to him, 'The best thing you can do is burn those,' and he turned round to me and said, 'The only thing I'm doing is burning the maggots off.'

One Christmas, this air marshal came into the sappers' dining tent to inspect the food, and one of the sappers threw his plate, and it hit this air marshal slap in the back. And all the gravy ran down the back of his uniform, and he turned round and looked, and everybody seemed to have a plate beside them so . . . nobody got into trouble, anyway. I think they were objecting to the fact that the officers' mess had fresh food all the time and we had this cooked-up stuff, pom-potato it was called, different things like that.

Irving

* * *

The only thing that a lot did seem to complain about was the fact that the tea was very liberally laced with bromide.

Lesley Andrews

Lesley Andrews was 21 when he went to Christmas Island as a National Serviceman in the Royal Engineers. He witnessed five nuclear tests. His health is satisfactory.

* * *

Flies by the thousands of millions.

Charman

* * *

Apparently there weren't many flies on the island until the servicemen moved in and established a rubbish tip, and they got well established after that.

RON HUNT

Ron Hunt was 24 when he went to Christmas Island as an army pharmacist. He witnessed two nuclear tests. His health is satisfactory.

*　　*　　*

Basically it was just common houseflies – so many they used to have traps in the mess to catch them, which were a yard cube of netting, with a piece of meat or an old bone or something in the bottom, and they used to empty them every day because they were full, literally full, of flies.

CHARMAN

*　　*　　*

Of course you got flies, but then we had what we called Captain Flit coming across every day and spraying all the tent areas.

JIM BURNS

Jim Burns was 25 when he went to Christmas Island as a corporal air electrician in the RAF. He witnessed four nuclear tests. In 1979 he developed multiple sclerosis.

*　　*　　*

The Auster aircraft used to go over at about eight o'clock in the morning, and you'd have sort of cornflakes and paraffin and DDT, which would float down on your cornflakes and your tea.

HUNT

*　　*　　*

Anything underneath, whether you were walking there or not, you got sprayed. If you were out, that was it; if you saw him coming then you could dive into a tent and you were okay. DDT, I mean you could smell that . . .

BURNS

*   *   *

And you'd go back to your tent after breakfast and knock the flies off the bed, and that was it for the day, and they used to fly over the next day.

HUNT

*   *   *

Millions of rats. If we left a Cadbury chocolate out they'd have it at nights.

COLLINS

*   *   *

We had steel lockers which helped keep our clothing free from the rats, because we did have rats – although that sounds far worse . . . The ones that we had were extremely small, and you could mistake them for mice, in fact. And they lived amongst the tents quite happily. We didn't disturb them very much and they didn't disturb us very much.

McLENNAN

*   *   *

Kangaroo rats that would pinch anything that you'd got to hand and leave you a stone for it. They'd swap anything for anything, pretty well, but you nearly always got left stones for things they took away. If you'd left a piece of food, or an odd sock or anything, lying around, they'd pick it up and take it away and they'd leave you a stone for it; and apparently this is the common thing. I'd never heard of it before, and I've never heard of anybody else having met them except on Christmas Island. A lot of the boys used to keep them as pets. They were quite tame – you could pick them up and handle them; they were quite friendly. They hopped, rather than ran like normal

51

rats. I don't think they were marsupials. I never got close enough to want to see, to be honest!

CHARMAN

*   *   *

The most common species of local fauna consisted of two types of crabs, one being a large roundish type which was easily noticeable whether it was left- or right-handed by the size of its huge claw, and the other a rather flattened type, green in colour, which when angered (which was often as we chased them out of the tent) would spit a stream of liquid at its attacker. We were later issued with proper service beds and mosquito nets but the beds still had to be raised to keep the crabs out. The green crabs were capable of climbing up material that hung from the beds.

BARRY COTTON

Barry Cotton was posted to the island as an RAF corporal electrician. He was 25.

*   *   *

The crabs used to walk up the side of the tent and get so far and drop on top of you in the night, y'know.

MICHAEL TIPLADY

Michael Tiplady was 19 when he went to Christmas Island as a National Serviceman in the RAOC. His health has been satisfactory.

*   *   *

They were very big crabs, big land crabs ... bigger than dinnerplates, and you could feel them, actually *hear* them, running across you ... And I think they done this for devilment ...

MCGINLEY

*   *   *

52

Nothing was said officially. Of course we knew about A-bombs (and this particular one was an H-bomb in fact), we knew about neutrons and protons and radio-activity from what you read about Hiroshima and Nagasaki and that sort of thing and pick up in the technical press. But there was no actual briefing about the implications of the test we were actually close to, at the time.

TREVOR SIMMONS

Trevor Simmons was a junior technician airframe fitter with 58 PR Squadron, RAF. He was 21. He stayed only a few weeks and witnessed one nuclear test. His health is satisfactory.

*   *   *

What happened was, we had two trial runs. And we got up at about four o'clock in the morning and we walked approximately a mile or so from the main camp on the road to the port camp, and just sort of sat beside the road. And at first light, which would be about seven o'clock, the first Canberra bomber took off, and then the second Canberra took off behind it – the second Canberra was for checking the instruments of the first, which was going to drop the bomb. And they did a couple of circuits, and then on the third circuit they came over the top of us, and there was a Tannoy system, and the chappy on the Tannoy system just said, 'This is a trial run.' And we just marched back to the camp and went and had breakfast and just did a day's work. And we did that twice.

IRVING

*   *   *

I'd been there I think it was only three weeks, when the first bomb went off. And I remember getting up, three o'clock in the morning, going down and having breakfast, and everybody piling onto coaches and driving down to the port, and . . . of course it was a big laugh then, driving down to the port, and the natives at the port area were all doing the hula-hula and everything – one big joke. We got to the port. Everybody got off the wagons. Just stood around. They told us then, 'Right you are, it's getting near time,' and we got onto these Ducks, ready to drive out to sea, just in case anything went wrong. But of course nothing did. And they told us then, the reason for that was, when the plane took off, that was the most dangerous time, in case it crashed.

BURNS

*   *   *

The lorries roll up, we are transported to the plain next to the coconut plantation. We (naval personnel) are dressed in shirts, shorts, sandals and caps. Army and RAF personnel are similarly dressed. We debus and form up in our sections and a head count is taken. We are all chattering and joking about the bomb. The lorries are parked near us ready for a quick getaway. (It's a half-hour drive to the port and with thousands of men to evacuate you can guess what would happen in the event of a mishap!!!)

COTTON (letter)

*   *   *

They did one or two trials, dummy runs. Suddenly they said, in the same monotone: 'This is a live run.' And then they said: 'Bombs gone.' The same way, same voice, same sort of thing so you were used to it. And then of course you had a 30-to-one countdown, thinking about this thing coming down towards you. And I can't help but remember that my feelings at that time, because I realised how flat Christmas Island was . . . Ten to 15 feet above sea level, possibly going up to a hill of 30 feet, which I never really knew where it was . . . And they said this thing was going to be exploded high up in the air so it would be a clean bomb, i.e. didn't bring up a lot of water or earth or whatever was underneath, I assume water because we were on the island . . . I thought that if it did in fact not detonate at the level they were hoping and went further down it would produce a tidal wave; and I didn't think a lot of our chances if it did.

McLennan

*   *   *

I think we had sunglasses on, you know, dark glasses. We had to cover our hands over our eyes. We were backs to the blast. And you could actually see through your hands. You could actually see, y'know, bones and everything.

Tiplady

*   *   *

The moment it was zero . . . I'll never forget this, the impression, you know, at so many miles away, was this tremendous sort of high temperature, heat, instantaneous heat from all that distance. And it took us completely by surprise because we didn't expect this.

Simmons

*   *   *

It was rather frightening when they set the bomb off, like, you know. I'd never seen an explosion before, or heard one. And it was rather frightening. We'd got no protective clothing as such. Just shorts and short-sleeved shirts, that's all we had, and a pair of sunglasses.

Edkins

*   *   *

After a few seconds over the public-address system came the instructions, 'You can now stand up and view the fireball.' And highly spectacular it was too. You saw the fireball rising up, orange, molten, all colours, and gradually turning into a mushroom. And all the concentric vapour waves, like ripples on a pond, spreading out at the speed of sound. And it was, you know, a superb adventure. A spectacle.

Simmons

55

For want of a better word, I'd say blasé about it. Everything that was coming to me, everything I was expecting. So nothing untoward happened. And when I turned round and looked to sort of see the fireball developing and the crown mushrooming up, all this I was expecting to see.

PATRICK TALL

> *Patrick Tall was 37 when he went to Christmas Island as flight engineer in a Shackleton squadron. He witnessed three nuclear tests. He has had operations for a stomach ulcer and for throat cancer, for which he is still receiving radiotherapy.*

*   *   *

Strange! Haven't heard a bang yet, has it gone wrong? No, the commentator's still counting, one, two, three, four, five . . . God, it's getting hot on the back of my neck, hot, hotter, bloody hell . . . six, seven, eight . . . some screams nearby, the heat recedes . . . 'nine, ten . . . 20 . . . 50 . . . 60 . . . Clear the trees.' Everyone rushes forward, turns and looks back. There's the familiar mushroom rising in mid-air. It isn't picturesque like the newsreels show. It's black, blue, grey, red, orange, yellow plus any other colour you can think of. They're boiling, burning, mingling, changing shapes all the time and you can imagine the heat involved, the air itself must be burning.

Strange we've still not heard a bang! Look how the cloud around the bomb has formed a ring, rather like a ripple when a stone is dropped into a pond. The cloud line is moving outward, towards us – BANG – the cloud line and the sound wave had reached us. Some men hit the deck with loud cries and tried to dig through the sand and coral to make a foxhole, but it was unnecessary because it was all over. Just a vanishing cloud line, a boiling bomb mushroom moving, slowing, slantwise in the upper air stream, and thousands of birds screaming.

COTTON (letter)

*   *   *

We just all went down. It was a colossal explosion. Which I suppose a million tons of TNT would be. However far away you are.

McLennan

*   *   *

He says 'Blast now', and we were all turned away from the blast, and then we were told to turn round and look at it, and we saw this huge big mushroom like everybody sees, and . . . Even then it wasn't frightening to me, we were only boys, we were adventurous, I mean why should we be frightened at 21 and 22?

Collins

*   *   *

At the time, the only reaction was I thought, God, I'm going home after this after all! But at the time I didn't think I was going to. I mean, I thought, 'God, this is definitely it!' But then of course it was a big anticlimax after that, because they said, 'Right-ho, back onto the trucks again,' and then back to work.

Irving

*   *   *

Working-day work, sort of business, we had two cooks in a shift, and we was cooking for 600 people, and the start of the shift we had to peel all our own potatoes, because the whole year we was there, we did have a potato machine but it was broken down when we arrived; after about three months they got it repaired but it only lasted about a fortnight and it broke down again. So when it was your duty this particular day you really had to work hard because you was doing a soup, dinner and sweet lunchtimes and evening. So you never seemed to get a break.

Taylor

*   *   *

The bulldozers, we used to have two. One'd get red-hot and you'd shove him in the oggin to cool down and you'd drive the second one in the afternoon, because of the heat ... You couldn't touch it with your hands, because it was so hot.

GILLMAN

*   *   *

Oh, there was drinking water a-plentiful on Christmas Island because outside the HMS *Resolution* mess hall there was a cooler system. And this is where you get your cool water from. Everybody always liked to drink iced water, when you're working especially. Used to jump off your tractor and run down and have a drink and then run away again.

McGINLEY

*   *   *

For drinking purposes it used to come by ship, but for washing facilities, used to have an old tanker, used to go down to the lagoon and fill it up, and then bring it back and top the tanks up above the ablutions and across in the galley for washing food, sort of thing, y'know.

TAYLOR

*   *   *

As more people came onto the island, there was a drastic shortage of water. There were two tanks. And – we sometimes did six, seven, eight-hour shifts; in fact before the first test we were working twelve hours a day. But the Air Force, who had certain tent-lines, were only doing six-hour shifts, and they'd take all the water.

So I was summoned to the squadron office one morning and the major told me to get in the jeep and he took me to an area quite close to the main camp, and he had some stakes in the back and he said, 'Knock a stake in there, knock a stake in there and dig until you find water.' I had a gang of Gilbert and Ellis Islanders, about 15 or 20 of them, and we pick-and-shovelled through the coral, which is like concrete, and then once you've broken it up it just goes into sand. There was such a panic, because there was no water . . . I had to shore up the sides of the trench as we went down. One day the major came along and said, 'Well, it's taking far too long.' And so he told me to take out the sheeting. And what happened, the whole thing fell in again. So he went off in a bit of a mood. And so we re-did it. And then once the water was there, it was starting to go a funny green colour so I decided to cover it. He came down to inspect it and said it didn't need covering. And of course when it all went green he decided it did need covering.

IRVING

*   *   *

Everybody was working, you see. On Christmas Island there was four or five to a tent. Maybe two guys was asleep because they'd worked through the night, and you three guys was out through the day . . . and then you come in after a day's work, flop out, they'd be getting reading to go to work. It was just work, all the time, really. No sightseers or hangers-on. Everybody had a job.

GILLMAN

*   *   *

The chap I worked for . . . He lived at Canterbury, in Kent . . . and he was one of these chaps, you could never satisfy him, no matter what you did, y'know. In fact while I was out there I had two weeks leave at Hawaii, and the night I was due to come back from Hawaii, I sat on my bunk and cried my eyes out. The thought of – not of going back to the island but going back to work under him!

TAYLOR

*   *   *

They had certain water holes in different parts of the island, with one or two sappers running them, out in the sticks, and they were mainly trenches not too far from the lagoons and the water had just seeped through and it was just about drinkable.

IRVING

* * *

No, there was no women on the island other than the Gilbertese villagers who, they'd a small village down at the Port Camp. And of course you were under the severest penalty if you went into the area at all without authorisation.

McGINLEY

* * *

It was very primitive. There was the Gilbertese on Christmas Island . . . the guys was built like Garth of the *Daily Mirror*; the women used to put this flower in their hair, but they used to put coconut oil on their skin, and stinked to high heaven . . . And that was Christmas Island . . .

GILLMAN

* * *

We used to have to cut our own hair. There were no hairdresser, y'know. Used to cut each other's hair . . . Just wear a pair of flip-flops, pair of shorts, and that was your dress for the day. It were just accepted, we just did as we liked, to a degree. And that were the best part about it, I suppose, we hadn't got the regimentation, like you did normally. Because I remember a big officer coming out from England once, and our captain, which was Captain Gooch . . . Captain Cooch, that's right . . . he says, 'I'm too ashamed to let you go on parade and see him,' he says, 'Go to work,' he says, 'I'll go and make some excuse,' he says. They were a load of rabble.

TIPLADY

* * *

The stevedores . . . I was posted down to the port camp to do some cable-laying, and I'd heard there was a roughish mob of sappers down there that were stevedores, and so the first morning, I went for breakfast and these chaps were in the marquee, which had open sides, just had a roof to it, and they were just eating breakfast and whatnot, and so when the sergeant in charge of this – I don't know what you'd call them, a mob, I suppose – decided to get them on parade, when these were stood in line, there were some with no clothing on at all, but just their bush hats. Some had got boots on and nothing else; some had got shorts on. There wasn't one correctly dressed, and each one was holding a mug of tea. They looked pretty odd if they'd got sort of sweat rashes in different places, and it was quite amusing . . . But they were a hard bunch, and they worked really hard, and they did a hard job, and they sort of lived hard, and probably drank hard as well.

IRVING

*　　*　　*

Great bunch of lads, right enough, but as you say, tough. And could they drink! They could drink with the best of them. And . . . I would say that when they worked, unloading these ships, there was nobody could touch them, the way they unloaded. And it was non-stop work too. And . . . I was quite proud. They were all Engineers, and really, we actually ruled the island.

McGINLEY

*　　*　　*

You buy a can of beer there and when you opened it, you lost half of it, because I think half the trouble was, it came out in a refrigerated ship, it was unloaded at the port, stood on the dock, went into the refrigerator there, came out of the re-frigerator there, stood around a while, then up to the Naafi, into their fridge, and then out again – and it wasn't worth drinking.

BURNS

*　　*　　*

The ship used to come in with the beer and, oh, it would be just sit there . . . Because they were that bored, there was nothing to do, y'know. Blokes just lay on their beds night after night. We had got an open-air cinema, but you just got fed up with going to the cinema. You go down and sit at the Naafi every night, just drinking, y'know. And that's what it was: smoke and drink, smoke and drink. Day in, day out. There was nothing else.

TIPLADY

*   *   *

One tune that was banned there was, 'How'dja like to spend Christmas on Christmas Island?' Because they played it one time in the cinema, and they went mad and wrecked it. Not that there was much to wreck but . . . they wrecked it anyway. They tore the corrugated sheets, they threw the seats through the screen – the whole lot. Then they had to rebuild it.

BURNS

*   *   *

You weren't allowed to swim in the sea as such, because the reef itself was dangerous. You could paddle in restricted areas. If you wanted to go swimming you had to go into the lagoons, which – although they had anti-shark nets up, they didn't exist any more, so really the sharks could swim wherever they wanted to. There were a couple of guys drowned [in the lagoon] just after I got there. If I'm honest about it, they were fooling around, and people just thought they were fooling around when they were drowning.

ROSS

*   *   *

Very shortly after we arrived – in fact it was a day or two – one of our chaps was drowned in the sea. And this was most unfortunate because they had lifesaving equipment along the beach (and the beach was right by our tents), and of course,

62

because of no instructions otherwise, people went into the sea to cool off, thought nothing of it. But afterwards we realised that there was two or three feet of water just immediately as you went in, and then there was the barrier reef which was very close to the edge, but a hundred fathoms or thereabouts the other side. And the Pacific rollers were coming in, hitting that reef, and of course quite an undertow. One of the chaps got into trouble, and they threw the line, with the buoy on it, to him, but that heat, the lines were rotted and . . . From then on, all swimming was banned in that area, and possibly had been banned previously; but it took us to lose a life to realise it was a dangerous area. Because none of the people we relieved were there when this happened . . . Well, I assume they couldn't have passed on the word, presumably at officer level. There were certainly no notices up.

MCLENNAN

*   *   *

Well, we was coming back out from Christmas Island to the *Messina* in a boat . . . only a twelve-foot putt-putt thing, small boat. And we were being followed out, luckily, by a man called Barry O'Brien, in a pinnace, 52-foot pinnace. And I remember we came out, we went over a couple of bits of this swell. One or two lads said, 'Oh, that's great! Let's have another one or two of them,' y'know. Anyway, the next thing we know, God! We seemed to be going up a mountainside, y'know, and then suddenly – *wallop*! Down we come. And I reckon we must have come down 25 or 30 foot. Just *bang*! Straight down. Anyway, chap in the bow, he sort of stands up. As we're coming down he's standing up and bang! Straight through the bottom of the boat, down to his kneecaps. Anyway, of course the water started to flood in . . .

JACKSON

*   *   *

You did your own repairs (such as they were) to clothes, you did your own laundry (such as it was). The washing facilities were primitive: sort of like standpipes built in, and buckets; and because the climate was so good, I quickly got into the thinking that what I didn't wear I didn't have to wash. So I was running around naked most of the time. And there was no women on the island – at least we were told that initially – and then we heard about these WVS ladies who were looking after the natives at the other end of the island. Whenever we flew, I used to sort of . . . like singlets and underpants and then I put my lightweight flyingsuit over the top. When we come down I used to wash them all straight away and hang them up. And I was doing this one particular day, and one of the ladies come by. But fortunately my washing bowl was between me and her, and as she walked by I was sort of working and moving around, as it were, you know. From thereon I never changed my habits, I was just more aware of who may appear at any time at all.

TALL

*   *   *

Something of an island paradise, I mean it was all sort of rosetinted spectacles. I thoroughly enjoyed it, it had got disadvantages, yes, but personally I rather enjoyed my service on the island, once I got used to the temperature.

There was a lot of dragonflies on the island. When we were at the hospital you could watch them fly down the coast, about a hundred yards out from the coast I suppose, in a steady stream, for what – five or ten minutes they used to go, from left to right, down towards the main camp. At five or six o'clock in the evening, they used to fly back again. Hundreds of these hefty great dragonflies, about, what, six inches long? Cats used to catch them and eat them. Where they bred, or where they came from, was a real mystery.

HUNT

*   *   *

I'll never forget the accommodation we had, which was full of bedbugs. And we had a tent which had one great big rip from top to bottom. And we couldn't get any other form of bedding, or anything. The bedbugs, y'know – terrible.

We had some powder to spray on, try and kill 'em. They used to get in between . . . All we had were camp beds, you see. And they used to get in between the canvas. You know, they have you scratching in the middle of the . . . Well, we thought that was what was causing the boils and . . . things all over the body . . . We don't know, y'know . . . I've got no regrets for ever being out there. But . . . I wish I'd never have gone, but . . . you know, it's the . . . the thing that happened – I was only a National Serviceman, I had no option. Sent, and that was it.

TIPLADY

*   *   *

Monitored? You've got to be joking! I heard that people got these little tags for the X-ray things to wear. I never even *saw* anybody with one.

BURNS

*   *   *

I wore a dosimeter all the time, and when the bombs were going off we wore them.

COLLINS

*   *   *

We were just kept in the dark, we didn't know really what was going on, we just went about and did our job, there were no monitoring or medical tests or anything at all.

IRVING

*   *   *

We didn't realise that we were going to be able to see through our hands, we didn't realise there was going to be any heat, because we just weren't told anything at all about what to expect. So when the second test arrived, we were issued with these little protective suit tops, and the second one was far worse because we knew what was going to happen and we were given the impression that the first one being as bad as it was, that if we were given these protective suits the second one was going to be a damn sight worse. That's why we'd been issued with them.

IRVING

*   *   *

And also one test which apparently went wrong. We were told . . . We were on the back of lorries, once, and we were told that we could look at the bomb, and of course we all turned round to look. The blast came after. And there were blokes being thrown everywhere. And, you know, first impressions was, the officers was running and they were leaving us there, you know.

TIPLADY

*   *   *

I first witnessed the hydrogen bomb tests, which was eight and a half million tons, that was on the 28th April 1958.

McGINLEY

*   *   *

We had on white cotton overalls. We had a hood, but it was anti-flash gear, it was a kind of a cotton mesh. We had gauntlet gloves.

ANDREWS

*   *   *

The islanders – they had Gilbert islanders there – they were took away in ships before the blast. Every time they were took away. Sailed off into the Pacific, out of the way. And we were left there as guineapigs.

TIPLADY

*   *   *

We weren't given any protective clothing. What we did wear was our floppy jungle-green hat and our jungle-green uniform, with long trousers.

MCGINLEY

*   *   *

There was about a hundred in our group. And we were sat in a semicircle. And as daylight approached we could hear the aircraft take off, and there was Valiants and Vulcans and Hastings, Dakotas, all that type of aircraft. We could hear the roar of the engines and one thing and another. And being the fact that it was our first bomb, many of us were a little bit apprehensive as to how things were gonna be . . .

ANDREWS

*   *   *

Somebody who was in his safe area, tucked away underneath a lorry, somebody kicked sand in his face as they were going past. And I think he was rushed into hospital – this was about five minutes before the bomb was due to be dropped. A few frantic phone calls, while we cleared the sand out of this chap's eyes, before he could sort of be safe to protect himself from the flash, when the bomb was let off. So that delayed one of them quite a few minutes, till they sorted that out.

HUNT

*   *   *

The chap on the Tannoy system casually mentioned that the bomb had now left the aircraft, whereupon I suddenly felt . . . 'Start counting!' And you had the strange feeling that . . . you were just crouched there, and you couldn't do anything at all. I think then I probably knew what it was like when somebody was standing in front of the firing-squad, after you'd heard that somebody had cocked the rifle and you were gonna be *wock*. And one had a great desire to remove yourself or to get in a ditch or to get *some*where.

IRVING

*   *   *

Then there was a 20-second count. At the point of zero, I couldn't hear nothing. I thought to myself, 'Well, has the bomb gone off, or what?' And all of a sudden there was a slight rustling and a murmuring behind me, and I could feel the heat coming up on my back like an electric fire.

ANDREWS

*   *   *

It was that type of white-hot heat. Then the flash subsided and the heat subsided, and then on the Tannoy system they counted up to 20, it must have been about 20 seconds, I suppose, and we walked out across the road and turned round to look at the fireball, which was rising above the palm trees, the coconut palms. And it was broad strips of yellow and greens and every colour of the rainbow really; it was just boiling over and over, and expanding, getting larger and larger. And I suppose within 20 seconds the blast hit us. And it was somebody being hit from your toes to the top of your head, by a force which is just passing through you. Most of us, a lot of us were knocked over. Some of us fell in ditches. And I landed on the side of a ditch and trying to retrieve my cap from running in the water. And at the same time the explosion happened and it was a gi-normous, I can only describe it as a metallic clang, I don't know, a million times bigger than you ever hear in a thunderstorm. And then there were several other minor clangs. And then a lot of rumbling. And we sort of . . . those who were fallen over or knocked over stood up, and the fireball went up, and I suppose we stood and watched it, and within about ten minutes or so we were just standing underneath the mushroom.

IRVING

*   *   *

It was just white, sparkling. And you couldn't look at it for a few seconds because it was so brilliant. And then it started taking on the familiar shape of the mushroom. The stalk started to go down; it was like a giant fir tree, with the cones going down, and inside the actual mushroom itself it was all just like boiling black oil. In a way it was a terrible sight. Many men were quiet, and I couldn't understand the reason why. I thought to myself, 'Well, I don't know, I would have thought there would be some kind of reaction, but . . .'

ANDREWS

*   *   *

The heat was so tremendous, and it was frightening. Many men, including myself, were actually . . . I don't know . . . It seemed to kinda do something to your morale.

McGINLEY

*   *   *

There were palm trees, and we were in a semicircle, and it was just like a field of corn, how the wind would come through a field of corn. And we could see the palm trees gradually bending towards us. And then the blast hit us, and it hit us with such a force that, had you been standing, you would have been knocked flying, without a doubt. And . . . some men lost their hats, they went flying. And one chappie, he did stand up there, which was our squadron sergeant-major, he did stand up but unfortunately he did fall down. He was knocked down with the blast.

ANDREWS

*   *   *

I had a sinking feeling after watching it. *Immediately* after watching it, actually, you know, and it's a feeling which I never thought I'd experience again. But I didn't realise they had another two in store for us. Both H-bombs.

McGINLEY

*   *   *

I suppose the power of the bomb just about doubled the power of the sun on your back.

HUNT

*   *   *

As we were walking back to the camp, it started to rain; because as the fireball had gone up, on both sides of it the clouds just disappeared. It was like somebody taking a duster to a blackboard and wiping chalk off. And the clouds disappeared on both sides. And as we were walking back it started to rain heavy drops of rain about the size of a penny. I suppose it rained for about 20 seconds. And it was as if they were sort of flying on the wind.

IRVING

*   *   *

On the way back it did start spitting of rain. And we really did panic with that one. We had to run all the way back, because we didn't know if the rain was going to be contaminated or not. But later in the day we did hear that there were about 500 people trying to get into a small hut which was about 20 square foot.

TAYLOR

*   *   *

It landed all over my face and my arms, and I took my sweatrag out to wipe this rain off, and I had a large piece of rain landed on my forearm. And I looked at it, and it gave me the impression that it looked more like gin than water. I'd read about these Japanese fishermen of the last war that had been contaminated, so I wiped my face and arms off, and when I got back to the main camp I went and washed it off.

IRVING

*   *   *

We saw the bomb: it must have been about 60 miles away. The fireball, and the cloud after it. It was quite fascinating from the way that the cloud changed above it. The layers of cloud that there were sort of formed, re-formed, disappeared, re-appeared within seconds. It took a lot of energy to do that little lot and it was very impressive.

As for ourselves as aircrew on the squadron, no special briefings, no special information . . . Protective clothing: nil. One indicator was issued to the captain of the aeroplane, a little lapel badge which was not supposed to change colour from its blue or its red to the opposite, and it later on, on the flight, did change . . . Our main involvement in it, really, was that we were down to the south of the island; there's no other airfields down to the south there until you reach Antarctica; so we had to get back to the island; and the explosion threw up a line of clouds in both directions, east and west; and we had to negotiate that little lot. The Shackleton has no great ceiling and these clouds were big, thirty-odd thousand feet average and, you know, the main one going a mighty sight higher than that. And we had to go through it. They're all chucking out rain. It was just a continuous line of rain clouds. Some bits were not quite as heavy as others, it was a moderate rain in the gaps and heavy rain in the rest of it. So we were forced to go through it eventually. The old Shackleton's unpressurised and there's a hatch above both pilots, an escape hatch, and the rain pours in. The moisture, the spray I suppose affects everyone in the aeroplane.

I would think in the order of half an hour after the explosion the line was well-established. And I say 'well-established', there's no way that we had fuel to go and explore the ends of it. You know that it's not right at the time to do it, but you have no other choice. I wasn't the captain of the aeroplane, but I couldn't suggest any other way through the problem. I think we all knew enough about civil defence aspects of nuclear fallout to realise that this was fallout; it may not be the worst type of fallout but it was triggered off by a nuclear explosion, and it was falling. And probably involved in the rain. I could be

71

completely wrong. It could all have gone up and over the top, and this just a met condition triggered by the temperature. Pure mid-Pacific rain. But I have my suspicions.

GLEN STEWART

Glen Stewart was 20 when he went to Christmas Island, with the rank of pilot officer, as co-pilot in a Shackleton. He stayed only a short time and witnessed one nuclear test. His health is satisfactory.

*　　*　　*

We got back to the main camp and went into our tent, and we had a system of brewing tea in a can, in fact an old jam can, and we brewed up tea, I brewed the tea, nobody said a word. Everybody walked back from the actual explosion to the main camp, and we all got on our beds, and nobody said a word for about two hours. One of the lads was shaking, with shock. I think we were just dumbfounded with what we'd seen.

IRVING

*　　*　　*

As far as I know, it was supposed to have been an air blast, 800 feet up and quarter of a mile off the shore. I don't know, the figure's entirely rumour; and again entirely rumour is the fact that it missed; that the cameras set up to take the pictures, the rumour was that no photographs were taken because it actually fell something like a quarter or half a mile short of the target point. I wondered about it myself in fact, in that with an air blast, quarter of a mile out to sea, the centre of it, the epicentre if that's the correct word, I would have imagined would have set up range circles, and that the devastation would have given an indication of where the centre was. A few days later we flew down past the site of the explosion, at a thousand feet and the centre was very close to the beach, if not actually over the land. It was complete devastation, everything churned up, just mud – well, not mud but coral sand – gradually dwindling away

72

through the palm trees, quite obvious where the trees all broken and fallen until at about a range of five miles, very little obvious damage; which again was a surprise to me. I had imagined that if you dropped one of these things on Glasgow that Edinburgh would look a bit of a mess as well.

STEWART

*　　*　　*

And we saw then that part of the roof of the mess has been blown off, and damage had been done to the camp. And by the end of that evening, it was talked about – obviously, being on an island, word travels very, very quickly – it was said that the scientists had got all their calculations entirely wrong. And the bomb was far, far bigger than ever they'd expected it to be. The following weekend we took a jeep and we drove to the other side of the island, where the bomb had been dropped. And it wasn't long before we saw that a lot of the coconut palms, the leaves had all been frizzled up, with the heat; and then for about another mile or so a lot of the coconut palms had been knocked over but they weren't exactly flattened; and for about the last mile or so to the end of the island the whole lot was just absolutely flat.

IRVING

*　　*　　*

We were crouched down on the deck with our eyes covered. We were already wearing goggles, sunglare goggles; zoot-suits, we called them, they were an anti-flash, double-nylon coverall type, with two zips on them. So we were completely covered up, anti-flash gear, facing away from the explosion. At that time we were told we were approximately 25 miles away. We had all the VIPs on board, admirals and air vice-marshals from Canada, Australia . . . New Zealanders . . . all watching these tests. And everybody convinced that we were perfectly well-covered for this sort of operation. Only at a later date I saw actually on TV that men in the RAF and the Army on the

73

Christmas Island didn't *have* protective clothing. Some were just watching the tests in shorts! Absolutely incredible.

MAUGHAN

Geoff Maughan was now a petty officer on board HMS Alert, *the observation vessel at Christmas Island.*

*　　*　　*

We went out there at very very short notice, for that short period, because we understood there'd been almost a mutiny out there, in that the Engineers who were there, when they decided that the tests that we were involved with were going ahead – a somewhat last-minute change of plans, as far as we understood – we gathered the Engineers there had just downed tools and said, 'Enough!' They didn't want to stay out there any longer. I mean, the word 'mutiny' obviously is a strong one, but they weren't obeying the rules. And I think I can recognise what the problem was. We only saw the chaps who were already there for a very short while, but without doubt they were like zombies. They were not themselves, at all. I tell you 'like zombies', I don't mean that they had anything wrong with them; they were just mentally exhausted. It was very, very noticeable that the island was being run down. And we understood that the whole idea was to pull off *from* the island. And this was why the shock of the previous Engineers, they had got a date to leave, they were on the way in their minds, and then suddenly told they were staying for another six months. I think it was just too much for them.

McLENNAN

*　　*　　*

We were drastically short of medical supplies: we cadged from *everybody*, every ship that came into the port, every aircraft that went on the shuttle service back and forth to Honolulu or Fiji, they were all asked to sort of cadge supplies from someone or other, and we did have a pretty rough time on medical supplies. Pretty well everything. At one time there was 5,000 troops on the island and our total supply of cotton wool was about five pounds. The gauze was all used up for dressings, the lint had all gone . . . or no, we were down onto lint for dressings . . . and you shouldn't use that, because that tends to leave lint inside the wound, you know. We needed gauze, but it just wasn't available. All the medical supplies that came over, with Air Priority One, they'd be on Honolulu airfield so long you could hardly read the labels for the bird mess on them.

HUNT

*　　*　　*

Anything we had, we had to either have brought with us or get people to bring in from Hawaii. The Naafi provisions were absolutely abominable. Particularly when we first arrived. There were just very, very few provisions at all. We couldn't buy a bar of chocolate, it was that low, and we relied on things being sent in food parcels for anything extra than we got from the Army.

MCLENNAN

*　　*　　*

55 squadron RE . . . they was hard guys, dear me, like one day they was working the coconut plantation and cocoa or drinking chocolate was gonna come up in a big urn an' it never arrived. Anyrate they put up with it, but second day it never arrived and on the night time they tied up the regimental sergeant-major, tied him in a bloody chair! And said, 'Look here: tomorrow we want chocolate, or down tools! That's the bloody end of it! We don't mind working – we want watered and fed.' I mean . . . RSM! Going some, to tie the bugger to the chair. They got away with it! There they was next morning! And their sergeant stuck by 'em, bloke called Sergeant Puckey, name was, he stuck by 'em, and they got their drinking chocolate . . .

GILLMAN

*   *   *

While I was on the island, *Reveille* wrote an article that certain people who'd been involved with atom bombs or hydrogen bombs were likely to have deformed children, and there were lots of things like that likely to happen to them. So obviously there was a lot of very worried wives at home that were wrote; and chaps that were engaged, their fiancées wrote and said, 'Well, any chance of that, we'd forget it', and a load of them got a lot of Dear John letters saying, 'Forget the whole thing'.

IRVING

*   *   *

We had the rainy season, was about a fortnight. And I think that was about the only time it rained during the whole time I was there. And it rained very, very hard, and it flooded . . . in parts it was up to your waist. I remember I was instructed by somebody I had to go to squadron office to take something or to collect some papers or something, and I just had to wade through it all. But within about two days it disappeared. Everything we had was absolutely sodden. In fact we slept on a camp bed, and we had what we called bed boards – you got any type of boarding to get your bed about three feet off the ground. One of my boots was floating around, and we had actually three feet of water in the tent.

IRVING

*   *   *

You had to wash in salt water, basically, which wasn't very pleasant. When it rained it was monsoon-type rain and of course it was free of salt. So the standard procedure was to dash outside, with a cake of soap, flannel, and have a sort of fresh-air freshwater shower, which was very pleasant. And this we did after the test. And I can particularly remember, you know, the tests having been completed, we had a sort of monsoon-type rainstorm develop about three or four days later, and we all went dashing out and had this shower. And word quickly came around, 'We wouldn't advise you to do this, really, because there's a possibility that this rain that's coming down, nice as it may seem, may have been contaminated by radioactivity', of the test that's just been completed. There was no direct order, as far as I can recollect. It was just that people said, 'We wouldn't really advise you to do this, you know, there's just a chance that it might be a bit dicey.' Some people took notice of it, other people didn't; it wasn't as such a direct order.

SIMMONS

* * *

I was in a tent when I'd broke my leg, and lying in a hospital tent, and somebody walked in and asked me if I was cold. And . . . I says, 'Oh, it's a wee bit chilly right enough'. He says, 'I'll sort that out for ye, Jock'. He smiled and walked away. I mean it wasn't a stupid-looking smile, it was just an ordinary smile. So he walked away, and he come back, oh, five minutes later with a lit torch and set fire to the tent, and I was trying to scramble out the tent and pull out one of my friends at the same time. It just went up! In a flan of smoke!

McGINLEY

* * *

There was one chap went absent. He wasn't actually in my squadron, he was in one of the other field regiments. And he decided he'd had enough of this so he'd go on holiday. Anyway he went out into the bush and was somewhere near a lagoon, living rough. Some of his friends, the other sappers, were supplying him with food, keeping him in good order.

IRVING

* * *

Driving back from the main camp, I stopped and . . . to pick these two men up . . . and I asked them if they wanted a lift back to the camp, because it was five, six miles back, and they says, 'No, no. We're just speaking to my friend at the moment.' And I was looking around, couldn't see anybody for . . . you know, couldn't see anybody at all! I asked them who their friend was, and they says, 'Him, there.' And they were actually speaking to a telegraph pole. They had heard the noises, the buzzings coming from the wires and the two of them were actually holding a conversation with the wires. And the telegraph pole. I asked them if they'd like to come on, and they could come back for their friend, and they said, 'Oh yes'. So they jumped on the vehicle and I took them straight back. Reported it to the officer down at the port camp, and they were shipped home, I think within a couple of days.

McGINLEY

*   *   *

We had one sergeant, who wasn't in our squadron, but he — whether it was the shock of the bomb that affected him or not I don't know, but he cycled round the island and main camp on a bicycle sitting bolt upright and shouting orders to imaginary soldiers as if he was drilling them. Whether he was trying to work his ticket home before the next test or what he was doing I don't know, but he appeared to me to be mighty unstable. And in fact he did disappear.

IRVING

*   *   *

The only swimming was in the lagoon, which was about an hour's walk away. No transport to get to it. So an hour's walk across the very barren terrain in the heat that we had, you didn't go there very often. And certainly not during the week — which was a six-day week — because there wasn't the time.

McLENNAN

*   *   *

Actually, it was very monotonous. There wasn't that much to do. I've always liked classical music and we could borrow records from the WVS women and when I finished my night shift, most of the day I would just play records, sitting down and writing letters back home. I've never been that much of a drinker. I found out there that if you didn't drink, you wasn't much accepted, because that was more or less the only thing that they could do – just go down the canteen every night and have a skinful.

TAYLOR

*　　*　　*

We were sitting in the Naafi, which was just beside the sea, and a sapper threw an empty beer-can, and it hit a drum – oildrums were for waste cans – and it cannoned off this drum and hit a Navy lad on the head. And . . . whereupon there was a little bit of a skirmish, so the Navy ended up at one side of the compound and the sappers at the other. And we were heaving empty beercans at each other, and it got to the stage where we were out of empty ones and we were chucking full ones. Of course the RAF police arrived, who policed the island; of course the Navy and all the sappers didn't take the slightest bit of notice of them; and they drove their jeep right into the middle of the compound. And leapt out, about five of them. Whereupon the fire was aimed at them, and they leapt back in the jeep and drove off. And then we decided we'd have a truce and carry on drinking.

IRVING

*　　*　　*

A sergeant in the Army was killed. It was classed as an accident really but . . . A bucket was dropped on his head from one of the cranes. And we were told to get on our way, out the road, because there was a disagreement. But . . . looking at it today, it was pure callous murder. But looking at it then, we were 19 years old, we just walked away from the scene.

McGINLEY

*　　*　　*

There was never ever much trouble; the only time we did find we used to have trouble was when the Navy used to get their rum. If in any 24 hours we had more than 8 hours of rain we used to get what they called a wet-weather tot, which was a further third of a tot on top. At the same time, when this third of a tot was going, the Army and the RAF also got this. And where they weren't used to the Navy rum, those particular nights when it had been, down the canteen used to go bonkers.

TAYLOR

* * *

A friend of mine actually challenged a captain on the island to fight. And the captain had mentioned to him that, 'Before we leave this island, you and I will have the jackets off.' And both of them – without giving any names away – were Scottish; and the captain duly obliged just before my friend flew away. The two of them the jackets off, round the back of the tents and knocked the stuffing out of each other.

MCGINLEY

* * *

One sapper in our squadron who . . . he refused to get out of bed. He'd had enough of it. So the sergeant told him if he didn't get out of bed he'd get him out of bed, whereupon this particular sapper got up and thumped him. And absolutely flattened him. And when we were leaving he was doing 28 days in the cooler, and he was sitting in the compound, because the guardroom or the jail was a wooden building and it had a sort of a wire-netting compound around it just to keep you in. The punishment they had to do was carry stones from the beach, backwards and forwards, and make a garden out of stones, and once they'd done that they carried it all the way back to the beach, and once it was back on the beach they carried it back again.

IRVING

* * *

I believe that in order to get instruments focused on the explosion, focused on the actual bomb itself, which they had difficulty doing when they were dropped from an aeroplane, they wanted to suspend the weapon underneath four balloons. They were large versions of the wartime barrage balloons. There were four, one above each other, and they suspended the bomb on three legs of cable, rather like the legs of a tripod, on a camera. And it was our job to fly these balloons with the weapon suspended underneath it.

LYCETT

*   *   *

There was somebody had pinched the CO's car and careered off, disappeared off into the wilds somewhere. And nobody knew whether he'd gone *towards* Ground Zero or *away* from Ground Zero or *which* direction he'd gone. I think it took the MPs 20 minutes or so to find him and pick him up, and make sure he *was* under cover. Sort of a . . . suicide attempt, I think.

HUNT

*   *   *

We went up the road about six and a half or seven miles (from Ground Zero) and we sat in open ground, dressed in . . . I think it was long trousers, shirts, and hats and sandals. I think it was long trousers because it was fairly early in the morning, and quite cool. We sat facing away from the Ground Zero, with our eyes shut and our hands over our eyes, and our knees drawn up, and we waited for the countdown. When the explosion came, despite all the precautions we'd taken, you could see a vivid flash, like a flashbulb exploded right in front of your eyes.

LYCETT

*   *   *

Well, we were all very impressed; but having said that we were basically, when I look back now at 20 years old and 22 years

81

old, I think of them as youngsters, really. And the fact that we were of the impression that the government, or the Ministry of Defence, knew what they were doing at the time – you know, we thought we were quite safe!

Ross

*   *   *

We just looked on it as a rather interesting event in a reasonably boring National Service.

Lycett

*   *   *

On the words 'About Turn', we stood up and swung round. There was a bright orange glow almost covering the horizon. As we watched it turned a red brown colour. The glow disappeared and was replaced by a black mass which spread out at tremendous speed, at the same time it shot a column into the air. This column grew upwards, shooting straight through the cloud above Ground Zero. Whilst this was going on a veil of haze seemed to be spreading both up and out towards us. Then it hit us – a tremendous bang, rather like the noise a plane makes when it goes through the sound barrier only many, many times louder. This took us by surprise because we had forgotten about it in the excitement of watching the burst. The blast hit us at the same time as the bang, rocking us on our feet and blowing several hats off. The bang was louder than most of us had expected. I had thought that perhaps it would be a boom rather like thunder, but it wasn't. It was a really loud tremendous bang. Still, perhaps that was not so surprising because after all we were only seven miles away from the heart of the explosion.

Lycett

*   *   *

You were only kids, you didn't realise at the time . . . When you turned round and seen it, y'know . . . There's nothing like it. The thing itself, it were absolutely beautiful.

Tiplady

*   *   *

To be completely honest, they were absolutely terrifying. The mere fact that we thought they were controlled is neither here nor there. But when people look at a television screen of a film, in a cinema, and see an atom bomb, or a hydrogen bomb – they haven't got a clue. They just do not have a clue. These bombs literally filled everywhere. Everywhere.

ROSS

*   *   *

On the day of the blast, we found a crab outside the signals section who'd obviously turned round when the flash happened, towards the blast, and prepared to fight for his life. And when the blast came along afterwards it had blown the crab clean out of his shell, and left the shell standing there, empty, ready to fight.

CHARMAN

*   *   *

VICTIMS

Proof is not everything.

Mrs Pat Lane had no proof – clinical proof, that is – when she wrote to the Minister of Health in November 1961. All she had was a seven-month-old baby crying in a hospital cot from the pain of operations on both eyes. That, and a great anger that a terrible wrong had been done and must be put right.

Mr Enoch Powell was Minister of Health and he was in no tearing hurry to reply. It was four weeks before Mrs Lane got a letter from a civil servant. What it told her boiled down to this: everyone had behaved responsibly and no-one was to blame. 'I feel that nothing I can say will help you much in your personal distress,' the civil servant said. Too true.

That very day *The Times* ran an article on the drug Mrs Lane had taken during pregnancy. So did the *Guardian*. They came to much the same conclusion: thorough testing had produced no indication of danger. Thus nobody was in any way to blame for the consequences. Sorry for your trouble, but it's just one of those unfortunate things.

Mrs Lane didn't believe that, not even when Enoch Powell (though prodded by a groups of MPs) refused to set up an inquiry. Three other parents of damaged children – Peter Carter, Michael Carr Jones and Edward Satherley – couldn't accept it either. They couldn't accept that blind fate was responsible for the extreme deformities of their sons or daughters. They had no clinching evidence, no expert witnesses, no backing from institutions like the BMA, no support from the Ministry of Health, no experience of taking on huge drug companies, and no money to speak of. But they had ample commonsense and compassion, which shaped their conviction that ordinary people had suffered because someone, somewhere, had blundered.

84

In the end – after a vastly exhausting campaign in which the *Sunday Times* played a courageous part – some justice was done to the families of thalidomide children. In the end, those parents turned out to be right. But if we all waited for the end before we did anything, the world would be a wretched place.

So proof is not everything. It may be a goal, but it is rarely a beginning. What follows is about a similar beginning.

THE FRIENDS OF TONY CRAMPSEY

It came about almost by accident. In 1982 an ex-sapper called Ken McGinley, then 43 years old, met the sister of an old school-friend, Tony Crampsey, and was shocked to learn that Crampsey had just died of cancer. The cancer had spread throughout his body. Crampsey's doctor said that towards the end his condition had resembled that of a very heavy smoker and drinker, although in fact Crampsey didn't smoke at all and drank only in moderation. McGinley and Crampsey had served together on Christmas Island. Crampsey had suffered a severe and painful rash out there – so bad that he had to wear full uniform all the time to protect his skin from the sun, which made the rash worse. At the time, this was something of a joke to others: the only man on Christmas Island not in shorts and sandals. In 1982 his doctor tried to get a copy of his army medical records from the Ministry of Defence. It was far from easy; and when the documents were eventually released there was no mention in them of any skin disease or any medical treatment at all on Christmas Island.

Ken McGinley and Tony Crampsey had been part of a group of nine friends who had all gone to Johnston High School, Paisley, in Renfrewshire. They had all joined the Royal Engineers and had all been sent to Christmas Island. McGinley traced the other seven. No fewer than five had suffered a range of psychiatric problems, one had had two heart attacks and another was ill with bronchial asthma. The seventh didn't want to talk about it. McGinley himself was far from well. For nine men in their early forties it seemed remarkably bad luck, if luck it was.

McGinley wrote to the letters column of the *Scottish Daily Record*, told his story and asked for any other Christmas Island veterans to contact him. Instead, the paper sent a reporter, David Livingstone. He wrote seven or eight pieces for the *Record* about the veterans' experience, and each report attracted more response from men who were just as concerned as McGinley but had never known what to do about it. Soon McGinley and others who had served at the test sites – notably Phil Munn and Tom Armstrong – found themselves at the centre of this increasing response. It was an idea whose time had come.

HARD-NOSED OR WIDE-EYED?

In May 1983 the British Nuclear Tests Veterans Association was formed; it had little money and no fulltime staff yet it kept growing. By 1985 there were branches in many parts of Britain. (In 1984 Armstrong left and is now secretary of another group, called the British Atomic Veterans Association.) The aims of BNTVA are to get recognition from the Ministry of Defence that servicemen were put in hazard during the nuclear tests without adequate care and protection; to get proper medical care for those suffering as a result; and to win compensation for them and their dependants.

In March 1985, when its membership stood at about a thousand, the Association made the first serious large-scale effort to find out what has happened to the health of the men who served at Christmas Island and elsewhere. In this book, I have used 'Christmas Island' as a shorthand term for all the British nuclear tests sites in the Pacific and Australia, including Maralinga (in South Australia) and the Monte Bello Islands (off Western Australia).

One thousand questionnaires went out to these members, asking where and when they served, which explosions they witnessed, what protection and monitoring they were given, and what had been their medical history since then.

There are two distinct professional reactions to this sort of study. One is to dismiss it out of hand as a waste of time, without even looking at the findings, because its basis is not scientific. The other is to treat it on its merits, limited though they may be, and get out of it what you can.

For the out-and-out hardnosed scientist to accept a study like this one as in any degree valid, the questionnaires would have to go to a group of men chosen independently so as to form an accurate cross-section of the population of Christmas Island (the Study Group). And in order to measure the significance of their replies, it would be essential to ask the same questions of a matched group of men who were *not* on Christmas Island (the Control Group). Well, the BNTVA inquiry didn't use a selected Study Group. Every member got a questionnaire. Therefore the Study Group is self-selected: it's made up of men who came forward and offered to join the Association for reasons of their own, and this creates a built-in bias. Why did they join the Association? Perhaps because they were concerned about their health? If so, you can expect to hear back from too many unhealthy people. Unless, of course, the imbalance has gone the other way and too *few* ill people joined the Association (being so ill they lacked the will or the energy) in which case you get a picture of too many healthy people – too many, that is, to help form a truly accurate cross-section. What's more, without a Control Group there is no yardstick. How can you say 'These results are abnormal' unless you have compared them with another set of results which you know are normal? And if you can't say that, how can you prove anything?

That, in a nutshell, is the argument of the hardnosed scientist, and if you're not prepared to settle for anything but absolute, total and cast-iron proof there's a lot to be said for it.

The other approach is to accept that the study is not perfect, to take it on its merits, and to make the most of what it comes up with. After all, you can always make allowances to correct the fact that it's a self-selected Study Group, and even without a Control Group there are ways of drawing comparisons and making measurements. What's more, the sheer size of this inquiry gives it a certain validity. Many public opinion pollsters are happy to draw their published conclusions from interviewing a smaller number of people.

That being so, you may wonder why the BNTVA didn't opt to have a Study Group of 500 *and* a Control Group of 500. It's not so easy. The aim must be to compare like with like. How do you set about finding 500 British men who served in the armed forces during the 1950s in the tropics, but not at Christmas Island? Having found them, how do you get the right mix of the Services, the right blend of National Servicemen and regulars, the right percentage of officers and senior NCOs? It's impossible to get that sort of information without the co-operation of the Ministry of Defence. Only the Ministry knows who served where and when (and even *their* records can be a bit shaky, as we shall see later). The MOD has not been eager to share its information with any unofficial body.

So what it comes down to is this: if you haven't got the blessing of the Ministry of Defence, or a small fortune to spend on a nationwide hunt to find a Control Group without the Ministry's help, then it's impossible to carry out any study that is utterly and completely scientifically valid. That leaves a choice between sitting on your hands, or doing what you can.

*　　*　　*

And as it happens, a good precedent exists for doing what you can. There was another report of a study of cancer rates among Christmas Island servicemen. It was published in 1983 by that respected and responsible medical journal, the *Lancet*. The people who wrote the report are eminent in their field.

More to the point, their Study Group was self-selected, and they had no Control Group. Just like the BNTVA study.

If the *Lancet* reckoned that report was worth publishing then, the BNTVA study is worth looking at now. So here it is.

*　　*　　*

DEATH

When I began studying the returned questionnaires (and I read and processed all 796 of them) I knew what most people know about nuclear radiation and what it does to the human body. It causes cancer. Four times out of five, people with cancer eventually die of it. So the first thing I summarised was death.

DEATH FROM CANCER & NOT FROM CANCER

Of 796 members, 142 had died when the survey was made (and so the form was completed by a relative or friend).

108 had died of cancer. 34 had died of other causes, the most common being heart disease. These were not necessarily all recent deaths. Certainly they hadn't all happened in the two years since the BNTVA was founded. Some died many years earlier. That, of course, doesn't make the story any happier, since what we're talking about is a group of men who were much the same age 25 to 30 years ago: they were in the 18–22 bracket. Not all: there were a few old sweats of 25 and even some elderly men in their 30s. But the typical Christmas Island serviceman was young then, and therefore he shouldn't be more than middleaged now. So it's important to know how old they were when they died. Here it is:

Age Group	Number of Cancer Deaths
18–29	4
30–34	2
35–39	10
40–44	10
45–49	15
50–54	16
55–59	19
60–64	18
65 and over	9

(In 5 cases the age at death was not given.)

89

So, of the known ages at death:

> About 16% died before they were 40
> about 26% died before they reached 45
> more than 40% died before they were 50
> about 57% died before they were 55.

That doesn't look good to me. Mind you, we all have to die of something, and the sad fact is that, for about one in five of us, that something is going to be cancer. And although 57% of these cancer victims were under 55, that means nearly 43% of them were *over* 55. What's more, 108 cancer deaths out of 796 returns is a rate of under 14%. Is that so bad? It needs a little thinking about.

I checked the numbers of different types of cancers:

Brain	9
Lung	28
Leukemia	8
Bone	17
Lymph gland	7
Stomach	8
Liver	5
Kidney	5
Colon	4
Rectum	4
Oesophagus	4

There were two cases of cancer of the bowel, two of cancer of the testicle, two of cancer of the prostate gland, and one each of cancer of the tongue, neck, larynx and pancreas. There were also 14 cases which were reported simply as carcinomatosis, meaning that the entire body was affected. (The figures add up to more than 108 because some deaths were attributed to more than one cancer.)

RADIATION BIOLOGY: THE DIRTY TRICKS DEPARTMENT

The basic building block of life is the cell. That I knew. We are made of billions of cells and these cells keep dividing. That's life. No cell division, no future. Agreed. Radiation can do three things to a cell. It can kill it stone dead. Or it can damage it so that it can't divide as well as it once did; maybe can't divide at all. Or it can change its genetic working. (Piece of graffiti: *Radiation fades your genes*: all too true.)

It's the second effect that causes cancer. Quite a small amount of radiation can hit the cells so hard that they stop dividing. Later, when they start up again, they sometimes overproduce. Maybe they're trying to catch up on lost work; nobody knows. They make too many cells, and those cells make too many cells, and that's how cancers are born.

But that doesn't explain what happened to people like the survivors at Hiroshima or Nagasaki. Leukemias peaked there six years after the explosions. Do the radiated cells wait so long before they run amok? It seems unlikely. For one thing, any cell, whether irradiated or not, would surely be long dead by then. The cold truth is that nobody yet understands exactly how radiation makes the change that makes the cancer. But there is growing evidence that we're not looking at a simple one-step process. It's more likely to involve a whole series of changes, and that's why the interval between dose and cancer is so long, averaging 5–20 years in humans. (Some say up to 30 years.) There are lots of theories. Maybe the irradiated cell itself doesn't form the cancer, maybe the radiation just encourages other undamaged cells to behave that way. Or maybe radiation weakens a cell, lowers its immunity and that lets in a cancer virus which otherwise wouldn't have got past its guard. Or maybe . . . In the end, there are two things to be said about the way radiation causes cancer. One is that we know it's complicated; and the other is that that's about all we do know for sure.

On the other hand we know quite a lot about which parts of the body are most vulnerable to radiation. This goes back to the business of cells constantly dividing for their own very good reasons of life and health. On what doctors like to call the blood-forming organs, such as bone marrow and spleen and lymph glands, the cells have to divide at great speed, because blood must be made all the time. It doesn't take much radiation to cause havoc to bone marrow, spleen and lymph. The same is true of the intestine, because the cells that line its dividing tissues have to change very rapidly; and of the gonads (testicles or ovaries) which are obviously in the business of reproduction; and of the skin. That's the list. The blood-formers, the gut, the gonads and the skin: radiation hits them first and hardest.

TYPES OF FATAL CANCERS

Lung cancer dominates. 28 out of 108. Well, that's no great surprise. All servicemen smoke too much, it's a well-known fact. But not *all* these lung-cancer victims smoked. And what is not such a well-known fact is that many a death certificate that says a person died of lung cancer means that something else really killed him; lung cancer just finished him off, it being in the greedy nature of the disease that it keeps spreading until it wins, and once it captures the lungs the battle's over. Often a questionnaire came to me with a death certificate attached to it, and often the order of events on the death certificate told the same story as the questionnaire – only backwards.

Let me show what I mean. A man who had served at Monte Bello died in 1969, aged 50, of uraemia and acute renal failure. His next of kin had no doubt that it was cancer that killed him. You develop uraemia when your body fails to get rid of its waste products by means of urine, and the waste fouls up your blood. No surprise to learn that this man's kidneys had failed. But whoever filled out the death certificate was unusually thorough, because he added 'obstructive jaundice due to secondary metastasis in liver due to primary carcinoma of sigmoid colon'. So what had actually happened was that the veteran got cancer in his intestines, and the cancer spread to his liver, which led to jaundice, which overloaded his blood, and his kidneys couldn't cope. Uraemia was the bullet, but cancer pulled the trigger.

In the same way, several death certificates that nominated lung cancer as the cause of death also mentioned the presence of other cancers – bone, for instance, or lymph gland. Maybe lung cancer tops the list because sometimes it was the last straw. I don't think there can be much doubt of that in at least one case: a lieutenant-colonel who served at Maralinga and developed polycythaemia a couple of years later. The effect of polycythaemia is the reverse of leukemia: too many red cells in the blood, which can prove fatal. He struggled with it for sixteen years and finally died, officially, of lung cancer. Which he undoubtedly had. But not for sixteen years.

After lung cancer the types fall into three or four groups. At one end of the body there is cancer of the brain (6) and of the oesophagus, known to you and me as the throat (4). At the other end there are all the cancers of the stomach and digestive system including liver and kidney; they total 26. In between are the blood-cancers: bone (15), lymph gland (7) and leukemia (8), making 30 in all. Putting them together like that may annoy the specialists, but it seems sensible to me.

108 nuclear veterans, of 796, have died of cancer. Another 57 have had cancer or have it now, and are alive. Their types of cancer fall into much the same groups:

Brain	3
Lung	12
Leukemia	4
Bone	9
Lymph	6
Stomach	3
Liver	2
Bladder	5
Bowel	4
Colon	2
Testicle	4
Oesophagus	2
Neck	2

There were also single cases of cancer of the kidney and the prostate, and four cases of skin cancer. Six returns did not specify the type of cancer. (Again, the figures total more than 57 because in some cases more than one cancer was named.)

Once more, lung is the most common. Bone, lymph and leukemia total 19. Digestive system, 16. Compared with the cancer deaths, the number of cases of cancer of the testicle shows a big increase: up from 2 out of 108 to 4 out of 57.

WE DON'T ALL GO TOGETHER WHEN WE GO

So now I've thought about it, what do I think?

Life is a battlefield, that's what I think, and the Christmas Island veterans should know that better than most. They're not alone in facing cancer. So far they've lost 108 killed and 57 wounded, but then everyone knows someone who's gone the same way. What have the veterans got to complain about?

Look at it this way. The fair share of cancer deaths is one in five. For 796 men that's about 159. The veterans are up to 108 already. Cancer is by and large a disease of the elderly, commonest after 50. Most of the veterans haven't reached 50 yet. One reason that cancer catches the elderly is that they become a bit frail, a bit weak, they begin to lack the natural health and strength of youth. Nearly all these veterans were warranted by the Services to be exceptionally fit and strong less than 30 years ago. The years take their toll, we all know that, but you don't expect to find 40% of cancer deaths in men under 50, 57% in men under 55 – men whose families have only just grown up. Which is what has happened to so many Christmas Island veterans: they came home, got married, had kids, saw them grow up, and then – too soon – died. The total score is well below what you'd expect it to reach, sure – but we're only halfway through the game. If cancer can hammer the nuclear veterans so hard when they're still relatively young,

94

what sort of tally is it going to run up when they start getting old?

That line of argument upsets the orderly mind, I know. The orderly mind says it's unfair to guess at the future. Mere speculation, which can't be supported by data. So who said life was fair? Is cancer fair? Are statistics fair? The trouble with the orderly mind is that too often it lives in the past. Data means history. Data is the way things *were*. And the orderly mind is comfortable with rules based on the way things were. But things were *never* this way. There was never a Christmas Island. So what are we supposed to do? Stand aside and wait until the death rate has spilled over the top and the excess deaths provide fresh new data with which the orderly mind can be comfortable? Especially when we're involved here in two great medical mysteries, cancer and radiation damage? Total and complete scientific proof is a fine thing, but by the time we have it, all the veterans may be dead. And that's a hell of a way to prove your case, by dying.

THE *LANCET* DRAWS BLOOD (NEARLY)

The *Lancet* is a journal read by doctors. For me, the best part of the magazine is the letters section because it is full of warnings, observations and discoveries, often from research teams. The letters make up about a third of the magazine's contents, and some of them are so lengthy and detailed that they are more like articles. The 9 April 1983 issue had a longish letter called *Cancer Following Nuclear Weapons Tests* from Professor E. G. Knox and others.

The others were Tom Sorahan and Alice Stewart and they all work at the Department of Social Medicine in the University of Birmingham. (Cries of Boring! Boring! Hang about. That department has a great reputation for searching through mountains of medical statistics and coming out with nuggets of gold. In 1970 Stewart and Neale completed an investigation into the effects of X-rays during pregnancy. They demonstrated that even very low doses of radiation to the mother could be enough to double the incidence of childhood cancer: a discovery of enormous importance. The *Lancet* published that paper too.)

In a nutshell, the Knox, Sorahan, Stewart (KSS) story of 9 April 1983 is this.

LOST AND FOUND: 6500 TROOPS

BBC-TV's 'Nationwide' had enlisted KSS to do a statistical analysis of illnesses and deaths among men who had been involved in nuclear weapons testing in the South Pacific. In April 1983 KSS reported that they'd found evidence of an abnormally high incidence of leukemia and other RES neoplasms (meaning blood cancers such as lymphomas).

They knew from an answer to a question in the House of Commons that 13,500 men took part in the whole series of twenty-one British tests. (That included those in Australia as well as those in the South Pacific, i.e. the Christmas Island blasts.) They estimated that 8,000 of the 13,500 served on or around Christmas Island. Therefore as a baseline for their study they used the number of *expected* cancer deaths for those 8,000 men in the period 1958–1982. The crucial finding concerned one section of those deaths: the expected cancer deaths from RES neoplasms.

KSS had been given the medical histories of 330 men who'd served at the South Pacific tests. They knew that, theoretically, from 8,000 men they could expect 17.2 cancer deaths caused by RES neoplasms. However, when they studied the 330 actual cases, they found 27 deaths caused by RES neoplasms. (The breakdown was 16 leukemias, 9 lymphomas, 1 myeloma and 1 polycythaemia vera.) To find 27 deaths in 330 men when you would expect to get only 17 in 8,000: that looked pretty damning. But hold everything.

On 25 July 1983 the House of Commons was told that 8,000 was the wrong figure after all. The Minister of State for

Defence Procurement announced that for all 21 tests the real total of men taking part was now 20,000.

KSS went back to the drawingboard. They reported in a letter to the *Lancet* on 8 October 1983 that '. . . if the (new) figures were accurate the appropriate population for our mortality data could be almost twice the number we had originally been led to suppose.' Now, when they reckoned up the deaths from RES neoplasms, instead of comparing them with expected deaths in a group of 8,000 they were comparing them with expected deaths in a group of 14,000. The study had been diluted, if not swamped. KSS reported: 'There is no longer an excess of reported deaths of RES neoplasms.'

Never mind. Their work had not been wasted. For one thing it helped to provoke the Ministry of Defence into commissioning a fairly hefty chunk of research into cancer deaths among nuclear-test veterans (of which more later). And it gave me a valuable figure to work with – the total number of servicemen from those who took part in the South Pacific tests who could be expected to have died of all forms of cancer in the years 1958–1982. KSS had calculated this to be 146.4 deaths per 8,000 servicemen. I, with the help of my pocket calculator, made this 18.3 per thousand.

So, of every one thousand Christmas Island men – and that covers all three Services, ashore and afloat – 18.3 should, according to fate and the law of averages, have died of cancer by 1982.

We know that the BNTVA study included deaths up to 1985, so for the purposes of comparison that figure 18.3 is now on the low side. Let's make it 25 and say that this now covers the years to 1985 as well. 25 is almost certainly far too high but I don't want to take any chances. It's better to be too generous than too mean. And while we're at it, let's dilute the BNTVA findings somewhat by pretending that 1,000 questionnaires, not 796, came back to make up the BNTVA Study

Group – keeping the same number of fatalities, just upping the number of servicemen to a round thousand.

According to expectations, out of one thousand Christmas Island men, 25 should have been lost to cancer by 1985. The BNTVA study has shown that, out of one thousand nuclear veterans, a total of 108 men have in fact died of cancer by 1985. The difference is 83 – equivalent to the sum of cancer deaths you could expect from a further three thousand-plus men.

FIGURE IT OUT FOR YOURSELF

Carry it a stage further. Assume that, because the BNTVA Study Group is self-selected, it is slanted towards illness and mortality – so slanted, in fact, that upping the total to a thousand was not a big enough adjustment.

Okay. If the problem is that too many healthy men did not take part, let's include a few more. Let's include another thousand. Assume that they completed the questionnaire and said they are in good health. Leave the other figures for illness and death untouched, and just double the size of the Study Group to two thousand. This has the effect of adding 1,204 completely fit men to the original 796 respondents. That should take care of any bias.

Now then: according to expectations the total number of cancer deaths already produced up to 1985 by all 20,000 men should be 500 (20 times 25). But if 2,000 of those men – the enlarged BNTVA Study Group – have already contributed 108 cancer deaths, does this mean that the remaining 18,000 men have produced only 392 cancer deaths? It seems unlikely.

NOW TRY THIS ON FOR SIZE

While I was at it, I exploited the research efforts of the KSS team in another direction.

They had obligingly worked out the proportions of servicemen on Christmas Island in different age brackets, according to their ages in January 1958. As you'd expect, most were young. Just over 73% were then in the 18–24 age bracket.

KSS also supplied the expected totals for cancer deaths up to 1982 for these age brackets. The combination of these two sets of data provided some interesting information. For instance, I was able to work out that those men who were 18–24 when they were on Christmas Island were expected to account for 31.8% of all the cancer deaths that this KSS Study Group was expected to have in the period up to 1982 (by which time, if they survived, those young men of 18–24 would be 42–48, of course).

That fits the generally accepted notion that most cancers don't strike young men. Here we have 73% of the Christmas Island services population, but they're expected to suffer only 31.8% of that population's cancers before they're in their mid-forties.

But when you compare these expectations with the realities found in the BNTVA inquiry, a very different picture emerges. An exact comparison is not possible, because KSS were working to a closing date of 1982, as against BNTVA's early 1985; nevertheless they make a remarkable contrast:

Age range in January 1958	Age range (if survived) in 1982	Percentage of Christmas Island population	Expected percentage of cancer deaths in this population to 1982	Percentage of actual cancer deaths reported in BNTVA study of nuclear veterans up to 1985	BNTVA study: age ranges
18–24	42–48	73	31.8	40	18–50
18–29	42–53	83	40.77	57	18–55
35–54	59–78	11	49	34	60+

This underlines what has already become obvious. Statistically, young men – men under 50 or 55 – are supposed to be a low risk for cancer. Old men are supposed to be a high risk. Among younger veterans the BNTVA study found that cancer has raced ahead as a cause of death. Thus cancer is not only striking harder at this section of the population; it is also striking earlier.

I estimate this increase in cancer deaths to be in the region of 10–15%. It's impossible to be more exact because the estimate involves comparing an age-range of 18–53 with an age-range of 18–55. Obviously the comparison isn't absolutely precise. But it's very close. According to KSS expectations, the 18–53 group should have provided just under 41% of cancer deaths. In fact the 18–55 group actually produced 57% of cancer deaths. That difference of 16%, when applied to the BNTVA, would mean there are 16 or 17 excess deaths among the 108 cancer victims recorded by the study.

I said I estimated the increase in cancer deaths to be in the region of 10–15%. If, for the sake of caution, you take the lower percentage, and apply it to the total population of 20,000 nuclear veterans, you get a figure of 200 excess cancer deaths, all contributed by men under 55. The estimate is based on the assumption that at least 2,000 of those 20,000 men have died of cancer, and that at least 10% of those deaths were in excess of expectation. Expectation says men under 55 should provide about 40% of these deaths; experience shows they provide over 50%. The difference is 200 deaths.

200 deaths may not seem a lot in a world beset by mayhem and massacre. But stand it up against the official claim that nobody was at risk and it looks a lot less acceptable. In fact it begins to look fairly appalling. Which it is.

BORN UNFREE

Enough about cancer (for the moment). Let's move on to deformed children. If you're feeling strong enough, that is.

Deformities are an even bigger medical minefield than cancer. For a start, what *is* a deformity? Some doctors include everything that you don't find in a perfectly healthy baby. On that score, webbed toes are a deformity. Other doctors reckon that a deformity has to be something either present or lacking that makes a difference to the child's quality of life. They would ignore webbed toes but include, say, deafness or a squint. On the other hand deafness or a squint might be curable, in which case the deformity wouldn't make such a *serious* difference as, say, a clubbed foot. So it's not unusual for doctors to talk about major and minor deformities, although drawing the line between the two is not a job I would welcome; and I say that with feeling because I've tried to do it. Here are the results.

Out of 796 questionnaires, 60 reported children deformed or malformed or handicapped at birth. I've sorted those 60 into 42 who were severely or grossly deformed, 13 where the damage is less easily classified, and 5 who are mentally handicapped. Those who survived have now grown to adulthood, which is why there are no names.

There are also 13 cases of babies who had no obvious deformity but who did not live long. Some survived only a few hours, others a few days. And there are two cases which I can't classify: a daughter who was epileptic when born; and a daughter whose milk teeth, lacking enamel, looked like 'black spikes'. Here is the list.

Children born with major deformities or handicaps

(1) Girl born with hole in stomach and suffering from Bell's Palsy.
(2) Girl born with spastic arm and leg; became severely epileptic and eventually suicidal; hospitalised at present.
(3) Girl born with deformed skull; also cerebral palsy.
(4) Child born deformed and suffering Down's Syndrome.
(5) Boy born 'athetoid spastic'.

(6) Boy born with cerebral palsy.

(7) Child born with spina bifida; died at birth.

(8) Child born with spina bifida; died during operation.

(9) Child born with spina bifida; died on the same day.

(10) Girl born with spina bifida.

(11) Boy born with spina bifida.

*   *   *

(12) Girl born with severely deformed spine.

(13) Boy and girl, each born with extra fingers.

(14) Girl born physically disabled in all limbs. (No details given.)

(15) Boy born with two physical disabilities. (No details given.)

(16) Girl born with a deformed right hand – extra fingers; also mentally handicapped.

(17) Girl born with one leg shorter than the other.

(18) Boy born deaf in one ear.

(19) Girl born apparently sound, but her body did not develop fully as she grew: no breasts appeared and the Fallopian tube failed to develop.

(20) Similar case: girl's ovaries failed to develop.

(21) Boy born with brain damage: died after 3 hours.

(22) Girl born with severely abnormal blood vessels and gross deformities of her right arm and chest.

(23) Boy born with gross deformity of the feet: both were reversed, the toes pointing backwards.

(24) Son born with muscular dystrophy; died young.

(25) Son 'born deformed'. (No details given.)

(26) Boy born with both feet severely clubbed.

(27) Child born with 'genetic deformities to the right shoulder and both hands; internal defects; lump on head'.

(28) Son born with unidentified defect of the heart; also suffers from an excess of red blood cells.

(29) Child born physically and mentally retarded.

(30) Girl born with major heart defect; died at 3 months.

(31) Child born with 'abnormalities'; died after 3½ years. (No details given.)

(32) Girl born apparently sound but developed alopecia aerearta and lost all her hair at the age of 3; it has never grown back. (Now in her 20s and totally bald). Also suffered from Crohn's disease.

(33) Boy born with hydrocephalus.

(34) 'Baby malformed'. (No details given.)

(35) Girl born with severe brain damage; severely physically handicapped.

(36) 'Daughter deformed'. (No details given.)

(37) Girl born with cataracts in both eyes.

(38) Boy born severely handicapped both physically and mentally.

(39) Two children: the first 'disabled' (no details given); the
(40) second born with a hole in the heart.

(41) Child born with 'congenital malformation of head and femurs'.

(42) Girl born with malformed head; died after a week.

*   *   *

Other defects reported were:
 (1) Scan revealed deformed foetus; aborted.
 (2) Son born with 'nervous disturbance to brain, causing severe headaches'.
 (3) Daughter born with bone marrow defect in both hips.
 (4) Daughter born hyperthyroid.
 (5) Son born with myleublastic leukemia.
 (6) Child born with faulty hearing.
 (7) Son born with deformed ('twisted') little fingers.

(8) Daughter born with scoliosis (curvature of spine).

(9) Foetus seen to be deformed: abortion.

(10) Two stillbirths reported 'with genetic disorders'.

(11) Child born prematurely with deformed kidney; died after one day.

(12) Boy born with deformed little toes on both feet; also suffered from Coeliac Disease.

(13) Son died of leukemia aged 12.

*   *   *

In addition five cases of children born mentally handicapped or mentally retarded were reported.

*   *   *

Look at it from any angle you like, it's not a happy list. The unhappiest parts are those where the damage is beyond repair – which is not necessarily the same as the most obviously gross deformity. Surgeons can do a remarkable job of rebuilding or even adding bits onto the body; what they can't do is a complete rewiring job. So birth defects that involve something as serious as the central nervous system should count double. The study showed up 12 such cases: 5 spina bifida, 2 cerebral palsy, 1 Bell's palsy, 2 spastic and 1 Down's syndrome. It also showed up cases where genetic damage may have hidden its hand, so to speak, for years before it revealed itself. Such as the daughter who seemed a complete and normal child – until she was three, at which point she lost all her hair. It made me think: how many other delayed defects did *not* get reported because it never crossed anybody's mind that the seeds of the trouble had been sown – literally – at the moment of conception? It's not a pleasant thought for a father. He could be excused for pushing it to the back of his mind. So maybe the figures produced by the study *understate* the situation? It's a point worth remembering, just as it's worth remembering that a lot of other servicemen came back from Christmas Island aware that they should think twice before fathering any children.

That *Reveille* article made such an impact eleven thousand miles from Fleet Street not because *Reveille* was in the vanguard of sober and responsible investigative journalism (*Reveille* wrote for readers with the attention span of an adolescent butterfly with other things on its mind) but because the fear was already there, waiting to be put into words.

If we make jokes about the things that frighten us, that explains an item in the Christmas Island 'newspaper', a typed and duplicated handout called *Mid Pacific News*. The special issue produced as a souvenir of the megaton test on 8 November 1957 was padded out with squadron histories, the last one being an account of the work of the helicopter flight that ferried stuff about the island, including sandwiches for the boffins. The article ends: 'It is to our scientific friends that we address our final remarks. Gentlemen, your food comes through whilst we are virile, but you will surely starve if you make us sterile.' It was a joke – but sterility must have been a topic of conversation for the joke to have any meaning. Sterility wasn't the worst that radiation could do. The worst was genetic damage and that was beyond a joke.

SAND, FLIES AND SEX

There was a dreadful irony about the British nuclear tests. They took thousands of healthy young men away from all women for a year or more, at the very peak of their virility. If my National Service is any guide, what the population of Christmas Island thought about, talked about, dreamed about and hungered for was, above all, sex. The bromide-in-the-tea theory may or may not have been true. It was current at every camp I served in but I never met anyone who actually saw a dose being put in the tea urn. In any case, you couldn't make a bromide strong enough to dull the sex drives of five thousand national servicemen without leaving them too stupefied to get into their shorts in the morning. No, the awful irony of

Christmas Island is that it gave men nothing to think about but sand, flies and sex (and the greatest of these was sex) and then sent them home with a nasty feeling that having kids might be a terrible mistake. Certainly I met and talked with many men who had been very worried about the risk of creating a deformed child, were mightily relieved when the first birth proved to be normal, and then started worrying about how the child might mis-develop. I talked to some men who could never get rid of that fear. Some couples made a decision never to have children; some adopted children; some decided to take a chance and then discovered that the husband was sterile after all. Even if radiation itself did no damage to the men of Christmas Island, the fear of it did a lot of harm.

FADED GENES?

Back to the big question. Did radiation do any damage to the next generation? There are two ways of answering that. First by looking at the numbers of deformities at birth and comparing them with (if you'll pardon the expression) normality. And second by looking at the whole idea of genetic damage from radiation – which, you may be surprised to hear, a lot of people think is a myth. They think all that radioactive unpleasantness at Hiroshima and Nagasaki didn't do unborn Japanese kids the slightest harm. Others think differently.

'At present about two in every hundred (babies) are born with some blatant and severe malformation,' writes Anthony Smith in his book, *The Body* (Allen & Unwin, London, 1985). Not everyone agrees. A leading paediatrician told me the figure for major malformations or deformities is one percent, with a further one percent for minor malformations. In Australia, during the thalidomide affair, the figure 1.6% was quoted. It all depends, I suppose, what you mean by major and minor. Anyway, Smith quotes a 1980 figure for malformations 'observable at the time of birth' in Britain of 2.15% of all births, live or still. In 1966 it was 1.9%. I'll settle for 2%.

The nuclear veterans in the BNTVA study had an average of

slightly under two children. 796 veterans, 1592 children.

2% of 1592 is just under 32. So you would expect to find, say, 31 or 32 deformed children.

The BNTVA study reveals over 40 children who had been born with major deformities or handicaps.

What's more, it found most of them without even trying. The original questionnaire that went out to one thousand members didn't ask about handicapped children or malformations observable at birth or indeed anything connected with genetic defects. It asked how many children the veteran had had, when they'd been born, and whether they were in good health or poor health: that's all. Many people wrote in extra details of deformities at birth and so on. When it was decided to send a second copy of the questionnaire with a reminder to anyone who had not returned the first, a new question was added: *Please give details of major or minor deformities or malformations.* I wonder what difference it would have made if that question had been there from the start.

Never mind. 42 deformities instead of the expected 31 or 32 is still a lot of extra pain and suffering. Could it have been a longterm effect of radiation on the sperm of men at Christmas Island?

It could. Nobody has proved that it couldn't, and there's plenty of evidence in other living things that if you irradiate the father he produces abnormal offspring. It's known to be true of fruitflies, for instance. But who cares about fruitflies? Who can tell a deformed fruitfly, except its mother?

IT'S A PUZZLE

The obvious place to look for better evidence is Japan. And after the Second World War, teams of American experts spent years studying the first (and, let's hope, the last) large population to have suffered radiation from nuclear weapons: the perfect human laboratory. The genetics study programme in Japan ran from 1948 to 1954. In that time the American investigators amassed a huge amount of information about the children born to couples who had survived the atomic bomb.

In 1956 the American National Academy of Sciences with the National Research Council published its report. This found no increase in genetic damage to these children, compared with the children of control populations outside Hiroshima and Nagasaki.

'The absence of any effect,' wrote Professor Joseph Rotblat in 1981, 'is puzzling.' Rotblat was part of the Manhattan Project that built the first atomic bomb and he knows as much about radiation as anybody. He's right: it *is* a puzzle. The Americans (it seems) had looked at everything: the rate of abortions, still-births, infant mortality, even things like the sex ratio of children and weight at birth. Everything (they said) was normal. And that's been the verdict ever since. No sign of an increase in genetic damage in Japan, and if the Japanese didn't suffer, how can anyone seriously suggest that Christmas Island did anybody's children any harm?

'The great power and beauty of scientific knowledge lies in the fact that it is built on a firm foundation of doubt,' wrote Don Cupitt.

The Ministry of Defence has had no doubt. The Ministry 'remains confident that radiation from the tests had no measurable affects on the health of those who were present,' wrote Geoffrey Pattie, Minister of State for Defence Procurement, to Robert Banks, MP, on 14 April 1983. He went on: 'Thus none of those present at any of the British atmospheric nuclear tests were subject to radiation exposure at a level which would have resulted in any significant health risk.' ('Atmospheric', by the way, does not mean 'up in the atmosphere'. It means 'not underground'. The 1952 atom bomb planted inside HMS *Plym* – below the waterline, in fact – was, in MOD terms, 'atmospheric'.)

MICE AND/OR MEN?

Meanwhile a researcher called Nomura at the Institute for Cancer Research in Osaka University Medical School was at work. Over a period of fourteen years (1967–1981) he carried out a remarkably thorough series of experiments with mice, thousands of them. He used 2,904 parent mice, 12,905 live-born offspring of these parents, and 9,645 foetuses. He gave the parent mice – sometimes male, sometimes female – doses of radiation and recorded what happened to their offspring (who got no radiation). He found that irradiating the parents' gonads produced mutations in the germ-line which led to a large increase in heritable tumours and what he called anomalies (meaning deformities).

Until then a lot of people believed that radiation could cause genetic damage only via the mother. Nomura proved otherwise. Radiating the father's gonads and not the mother's could and did lead to deformed births. He found that the higher the dose of radiation, the more genetic damage resulted. No surprise there – the more you give, the worse it gets: a rule-of-thumb in radiation biology. But some have said that, to get any genetic effect at all, you have to deliver quite big doses, and Nomura showed that this wasn't so, either. With a dose of radiation as low as 36 rads, there was a definite genetic effect. The 'anomalies' included hydrocephalus, too many fingers, malformations of the eye or the body, and others more gruesome that I shall spare you.

You can't argue with 25,454 mice. After Nomura, there could be little doubt that, if you did to men what he had done to mice, the outcome would be very similar. Radiation not only fades your genes, it also shrinks them, stretches them, frays them, and splits the seams.

Nomura, in his laboratory, had done, over and over again, with fairly low-level doses of radiation, what the NAS report said had not been done by two Atom bombs. The world over, research scientists read his findings, and with some it was enough to shake their faith in the 1956 National Academy of Sciences report. In any case, that report was already beginning to come under fire, not for what it said – it's very honest – but for what it either didn't say or didn't take adequately into account.

TRACKING THE TRUTH

For instance it didn't take into full account the fact that in 1948 Japan was a mess. The war had knocked Japan sideways. There were serious shortages of everything from fuel to food, and above all Japan was struggling to survive without the hundreds of thousands of skilled men and women who had died in the war. (For every British civilian killed, Japan lost six civilians; for every British serviceman killed or missing, Japan lost five servicemen.) Life in Hiroshima and Nagasaki was very unlike England's own dear Home Counties, or the greener pastures of Long Island, and unless you try to see the Japan of those years through Japanese eyes you're in grave danger of getting a very unreal picture. How do I know? Because when I was travelling around Britain, seeking the truth about Christmas Island (the truth recedes as fast as you chase it, but the tracks it leaves are interesting) I heard about all this new scepticism concerning the 1956 NAS report. Some fairly gaping holes are being made in it by some quite eminent people. The work is complex and some of it is still incomplete, but I can reveal one new piece of evidence that, to my mind, throws into doubt all the conclusions that the NAS reached, concerning levels of genetic damage.

Given the nature of many deformities, a lot of deformed babies don't survive: either they are stillborn or they die at birth. Given the nature of Japanese society in those days, it's not surprising that the death of an infant was received with stoicism. Japan was a crowded little island. Infanticide had been practised within living memory. Few Japanese families would long mourn the death of a deformed child.

Remember that, as I tell you that in the period of the NAS study (1948–1954) more than a third of all the babies that died at birth were never seen by a doctor. So the American researchers seeking a statement about the appearance at birth depended on the only witnesses – the mother, and the attending midwife.

And the Japanese midwife of the late 1940s was not the crisp and competent figure we associate with British (or American) midwives. The great majority of Japanese midwives had received no professional training. They had been licensed under a pre-war system that set only one requirement for a midwife: she should have completed eight years' schooling. So a woman could have started school at 6, left at 14, and gone on to get a licence as a midwife. (Presumably she attached herself to an experienced midwife for on-the-job training.) What's more it's quite possible that many women who gave birth at Hiroshima and Nagasaki didn't even have the benefit of a licensed midwife, because in 1948 there were 110,176 *unlicensed* midwives at work in Japan.

This must mean that in the case of at least one-third of all infant deaths there was no reliable evidence about the appearance at birth. The midwife – whether licensed or unlicensed – wasn't qualified to recognise or identify defects or malformations, and more to the point she was likely to be more concerned about the peace of mind of the mother than about the statistical niceties of official record-keeping. Bad enough that the birth was a failure; why spell out the awful details of that failure on a municipal form? Better to comfort the living by forgetting the dead. I don't say that this *always* happened. Nobody knows. Which also means nobody knows how many deformations and defects went unreported in that one-third of all babies who died. So already there is an area of uncertainty big enough to cast doubt on the NAS report's conclusion that genetic damage was not excessive. And that's not all.

The data about the condition of live-born infants came from Japanese doctors, and such data has been treated as if it were reliable. But this is to assume that Japanese doctors then were like Western doctors. They were not. The war had killed a great number of Japanese doctors, and in 1948–1954 their replacements were young and newly qualified and very inexperienced. Often they had part-time jobs in something other than medicine. It would be dangerous to assume that they always recognised a defect or a deformity when they saw one, just as it would be dangerous to assume that they always got the chance to look – that every mother was willing to undress the infant for the doctor's inspection, especially in a cold house during a fuel shortage. So live births present an area of uncertainty too.

There are several other dubious aspects to the 1956 NAS report which are also being researched. We shall have to wait for the results of that work. Meanwhile it would be wise to remember the damage done when the effects of low-level radiation passed from father to son in Nomura's mice. It certainly works in animals, and as Joseph Rotblat has pointed out: 'There is no reason why the human species should be unique in this respect.'

GENETIC LEAPFROG

It is, of course, *possible* that Christmas Island wasn't to blame for any deformed or defective children. It would be nice to think so; more than nice, it would be a huge relief to a lot of fathers or would-be fathers. (After all, at 46 or 47 you're not yet past it.) Unhappily the story doesn't end there. The damage done by radiation to the genes might not show itself for *two* generations. This didn't occur to me until I met Frank Gray. He manned a landingcraft that ferried men and materials in and around the Monte Bello islands during the 1952 test (the one that annihilated HMS *Plym*). Gray is concerned about his three children, who carry either far too much weight or far too little, but he also worries about his five grandchildren. Two are normal. Then there's a boy so hyperactive that he has to be sedated. (Hyperactivity is often linked to a malfunction of the lymph gland.) One girl has failed to grow; after 2½ years she is the size of a six-month-old baby. The last-born girl has, in effect, no nose – the bridge is missing and her face is flat, with the nostrils up towards her eyes. All this could, of course, be chance, an unlucky roll of the genetic dice. But I can't blame Frank Gray for occasionally brooding about Monte Bello, any more than I can suggest to another Christmas Island veteran that he accepts philosophically the fact that, of his three grandchildren, one is okay, one is deaf, and one has Down's Syndrome.

It's not simply a medical problem – although God knows looking after a deformed or a disabled child is never simple: it's not just a question of using patience and wheelchairs. Deformed children grow up (or at least grow big). I came across a nuclear veteran's wife whose son is in his twenties. He is over six foot tall, powerful and active. But mentally and emotionally he is an infant, so he behaves like an infant, dragging himself around the house on his backside. It takes a special kind of dedication to care for a six-foot infant. However . . . That's not what I started to say. Christmas Island created two kinds of possible genetic damage. One you know about. The other is the damage done by fear that is felt by some veterans' children who are now old enough to have children of their own, and who can't help thinking that it might be a very bad idea. Such people are in trouble. They need help, and it's not the kind of help their local GP can give. However willing he may be, chances are that he knows nothing about radiation medicine. Very few medical colleges teach it and scarcely any GPs learn anything about it once they've qualified. The attitude of most doctors to the subject is patchy at best. Many nuclear veterans have found that it is worse than a waste of time to mention radiation to their doctors, because he not only refuses to discuss it, he does so in a way that says "For God's sake, don't waste my time with any more paranoid suggestions like that". It is only fair to add that occasionally the bias works the other way: one veteran actually changed his eye consultant when the man suggested the radiation link, only to find that the next consultant made the same diagnosis. But down at the grass roots, radiation is likely to be the very last factor that the average doctor thinks of. And even if he did, he'd be very hard pressed to know what to do next.

*　　*　　*

113

CATARACTS

On 21 May 1946, a man called Louis Slotin was in a laboratory in Los Alamos, experimenting with plutonium. He wanted to show his colleagues how the critical mass got nearer as he brought two hemispheres of plutonium together. He made a mistake, and used his bare hands to correct it. Slotin died. The man standing beside him developed cataracts. That, of course, involved a lot of radiation. But the lens of the eye is very sensitive, even to quite small amounts of radiation. As with cancers, there's a latent period. You get a dose of radiation in the eye, you go away and one year later, or five, or ten, the back of the lens begins to cloud over until eventually you can't see through it. The only answer is an operation. Eye surgeons who perform this operation rarely meet young patients. Cataract is 'virtually unknown as a spontaneous occurrence among young men,' said a letter to the *Lancet* in 1983. Cataracts are usually caused by old age; in fact it's rare to find them in men who are 40 to 45. Even in men of 45 to 50 it's very unusual.

When I'd finished processing the 796 questionnaires in the BNTVA study, I had a list of 25 men with cataracts. Seventeen of them were under 50 when their cataracts were diagnosed. Nine were 45 or under when their cataracts were diagnosed. Here is the full list:

Name	Age in 1985	Age when cataract(s) diagnosed	Interval in years between nuclear test and diagnosis	One eye or both
(1)	67	65	25	Both
(2)	47	41	21	Both
(3)	64	63	23	Both
(4)	56	52	25	Both
(5)	64	58	19	Both
(6)	49	47	25	Both
(7)	60	45	17	Both

114

Name	Age in 1985	Age when cataract(s) diagnosed	Interval in years between nuclear test and diagnosis	One eye or both
(8)	63	60	31	Both
(9)	47	46	26	One
(10)	49	32	12	Both
(11)	48	47	26	One
(12)	52	47	23	Both
(13) Died aged 53		41	11	One
(14)	66	66	24–27	One
(15)	56	55	27	One
(16)	52	49	25–29	One
(17)*	74	35	1	One
(18)	51	43	19	Both
(19)	52	38	19	One
(20)	50	46	23	Both
(21)	58	47	18	Both
(22)	47	27	7	One
(23)	64	52	14	Both
(24)	68	42	2	One
(25)	50	43	20	Both

*(17) was at Hiroshima and Nagasaki in 1946–48.

To paraphrase Wellington: I don't know what those figures do to the medical statisticians but by God they startled me. In fact when I first saw the number of people reporting cataracts I didn't believe it, so I double-checked each and every one of them, mainly by telephoning, sometimes by writing. Sure enough, a couple of cases bit the dust. However, when I'd discarded these mistakes I ended up with the list you've just read: 25 men who have cataracts or have had cataracts. And two-thirds of them developed cataracts when – according to the experts – they were in the wrong age-group. They were too young.

Let's leave aside the eight men who were over fifty when their cataracts were diagnosed (since age may have been the cause there) and concentrate on the remaining seventeen.

Cataracts tend to run in the family, so it was worth asking these men if there was any family history of cataracts. Only one respondent said yes – and in his case it was a grandfather who had developed cataracts in his late seventies. It's also known that diabetes can sometimes lead to cataracts, so it was worth asking about that too. None of the seventeen had diabetes before he developed cataracts. So we can virtually rule out prior causes or tendencies.

There was one final check. Cataracts can be either anterior (front of the lens) or posterior (back of the lens). The interesting thing is that radiation-linked cataracts are inevitably posterior. This time the check was not so easy. Often the seventeen men had had their cataracts treated so long ago that many found the information impossible to obtain.

But in five cases the facts are known. Two of these men had anterior cataracts; three had posterior cataracts. That rules out two cases as being radiation-linked. As for the other three: it doesn't prove absolutely and finally that they *were* caused by radiation; it merely increases the balance of probability that they were.

Cataracts in young or youngish men are rare; when they get posterior cataracts it is a phenomenon that demands urgent attention. Here is one aspect of radiation medicine where there is no need to wait until the individual is dead before collecting data. Research into cataracts can be done speedily and cheaply. Thanks to the BNTVA study I tracked down seventeen nuclear veterans who were under fifty when they got cataracts, and I did it in a few weeks. How many more are out there waiting to be found?

BULLET OR BUCKSHOT?

Eventually, if you keep beating your head against a wall, you make a hole in one of them. The wall I've been beating my head against is a wall of medical histories, and at last I can see light. Or are those stars?

Let's go back to where we came in. The cancer death total among Christmas Island veterans, as shown up by the study, is too high. The question on the front of this book – *So What's Killing Them Off?* – gets the answer: cancer. Not because the total has yet passed the 20% mark, but because it's rapidly getting there and far too soon; to do that it's been killing a lot of men who were well under 50, and that's too young. Something is going wrong to produce this result. (And it may be worse than we know. Given a high incidence of cancer, there's a risk that in some people the disease will weaken the body's immune system, thus opening the door to other killer diseases that would normally have been resisted.)

The same group of men – a sample of 796 from a force of 20,000 – has produced more deformed children than it should have. Death is death, but a deformed child is a blow to the heart. One is one too many. In this case we're not talking about one, we're talking about more than forty. Add that to the thought in the back of your mind and now consider this.

The same group includes 25 men who have had cataracts, most of them at an age when cataracts simply don't happen to men, some of them in a form that points strongly to a link with radiation.

Cancer *and* deformities *and* cataracts. All in the same group of men. All of them defects or diseases that are associated with radiation, all of them occurring in men who served at nuclear tests. Is it conceivable that this three-way effect is sheer chance? Well, yes, I suppose that anything is conceivable. But is it credible? Where does the balance of probability lie?

Radiation is not a rifle but a shotgun. This is the message that comes out of the BNTVA study. The dangers from radiation cannot be neatly defined and limited. Its spray of unseen, unheard, unfelt buckshot might strike anywhere. And this points towards the great difference between radiation injury and conventional medicine. Radiation is silent and invisible; you can't taste it, smell it, or feel it. Nor can you be sure what it will do to you, or even whether it will do anything at all. Our ignorance of radiation at any level is colossal. We don't know *how* it kills cells. We don't know *how* it causes cancer. (Radiation-bred cancers are indistinguishable from other cancers.) When it comes to the genetic effects of radiation in human beings, we know it happens, but almost all the rest is guesswork. Until recently it was assumed that radiation could induce cataracts only when the dose was received from the outside; now there is evidence that the bloodstream can carry radionuclides (nuclides that are radioactive) and deposit them inside the eye; in this way a cataract could be caused by radiation carried around inside the body. The more we know, the more we realise how little we know – and perhaps the biggest black hole of all in our understanding of radiation damage is the apparently random way it strikes down one man and leaves another untouched; or affects this man after ten years but waits twenty years before surfacing in that man.

This is what makes the concept of the radiation shotgun so important. Official reassurances about Christmas Island always focus on one trouble, one disorder. It's time to look at the bigger medical picture, to ask more wide-ranging questions. Which brings me to Didcot.

D'YOU WANT IT QUICK, OR D'YOU WANT IT GOOD?

I went to Didcot, and then went a few miles outside it, to talk to Dr John Dennis in his office at the National Radiological Protection Board. The NRPB is one of those giant agencies that nobody outside the business has ever heard of. The place looks like a small but very high-class university campus.

I went there because the Christmas Island affair – no matter how often Ministers reassured Parliament that nobody was ever at risk – refused to go away. BBC-TV's 'Nationwide' had started people thinking in 1982; then came the formation of the BNTVA; in September 1983 'Panorama' devoted an entire programme to the subject. On 4 October 1983 the Government announced that the Ministry of Defence had commissioned a survey of the health of the men who had taken part in the British nuclear tests. This was, Adam Butler told the House of Commons, in recognition of public worry on the issue, to be fair to those involved, and to allay family concern. The survey would cost £150,000 (or £200,000, depending which newspaper you read) and would be done by the NRPB. What nobody announced was that the Government wanted this thing done *fast*. And that was to make a great deal of difference.

John Dennis is Assistant Director of Physical Sciences at the NRPB. I found him, for a scientist, very accessible. He didn't try to baffle me with jargon and he didn't try to claim that everything would go perfectly.

When the NRPB got this job they published a protocol, which is a sort of draft statement of aims and means.

On page 1, under 'Medical Considerations', the protocol made two statements as if the second logically followed upon the first. What it said was:

'It is also generally accepted that effects may be experienced as a result of exposure to lower levels of radiation and that these effects may cause illness, most notably cancer, after the passage of many years. Therefore this Study will be restricted to an examination of the subsequent pattern of malignant diseases among those who took part in the test programme.'

Not much doubt about the first statement: lower levels of radiation can cause cancer. But the next word is 'therefore' and I didn't see why that should be. Because radiation causes cancer, why should the Study be restricted to examining patterns of cancer?

Dr Dennis said he thought I'd misread that part. (By which I charitably took him to mean that the writer had miswritten it.) What the writer had in mind, he said, was that because cancer

119

is the thing that's primarily associated with exposure to radiation, this was the thing which above all must be followed up.

COMPREHENSIVE, IN A LIMITED WAY

The truth of the matter is that the enquiry is going to be mainly about cancer. The NRPB is making a morbidity study of cancer (using the records of cancer sufferers who are alive as well as of those who have died) and also a mortality study which takes all deaths into account. Now, death is a surprisingly difficult commodity to measure. Dr Dennis and I had already exchanged views about death certificates, which (he said) are the most important part of the study because they are the most comprehensive record which is available, and available quickly, of any health effect which might be expected in any population. Knowing, of course, that death certificates themselves are not always completely accurate.

There, I suggested, he was being generous.

In 1982 Dr Hector Cameron, senior lecturer in pathology at Edinburgh University, reported to the Royal College of Physicians and the Royal College of Pathologists that he had found in 15% of cases a significant discrepancy between the cause of death identified by autopsy and the condition diagnosed by the patient's doctor. 'Significant', in Dr Cameron's vocabulary, meant that if the doctor had got it right when the patient was still alive he would have treated him differently.

15% is about one in seven. If that doctor completes the death certificate, it seems reasonable to assume that he would confirm his mis-diagnosis on that document. As Dr Cameron pointed out, the proportion of autopsies performed in hospitals fell from 60% of deaths in 1967 to 20% in 1982. So the opportunity for correction comes relatively seldom. Therefore – I put it to Dr Dennis – how can you trace all ex-servicemen from Christmas Island who died of cancer when the doctor may have put down broncho-pneumonia?

Well, as I said, Dr Dennis was not about to claim perfection. But he pointed out that death certificates are more informative

120

than I implied. There's more than one cause of death indicated, he said, and gave the hypothetical example of a man knocked down by a bus who at the same time is suffering from cancer. You may well find cancer mentioned on the death certificate as well. All those subsidiary causes, he said, are put into the NRPB computer programmes.

This is where I expected him to play his ace: the national cancer registry, which is a project run by the National Health Service, to record every cancer patient and victim in the country. It turned out to be more of a jack than an ace. 'Over the period of years it has got much better,' he said, 'but in the early years, particularly the years following the 1950s, the 1960s where we might be concerned, not all the morbidity records are as complete as we would like. So it's not quite so good as the death certificates in terms of completeness.'

There was another statement in the protocol that had made me pause and stare into the distance. It was about lung cancer. Now, the study is doing a whole array of analysis – all causes of death combined, all cancers, all solid malignant tumours, all leukemias, and so on. However, it will consider lung cancer separately because it expects that type to be the biggest single component of all cancers. No quarrel there. But it goes on to say that 'interpretation of any findings will be difficult since it is likely that both the Study and the Control Group will contain large numbers of heavy smokers.' That looked to me like something of a pre-emptive strike by the writer of the protocol. Sort of: Don't blame us if the outcome is blurred by tobacco smoke.

'Well, it's certainly going to be blurred,' Dr Dennis said, 'but I would contest whether we'd be unable to draw a valid conclusion, because quite obviously if any exposure to radiation or any other carcinogenic agent during the course of the tests has increased the lung-cancer incidence among those people who served there, it will show up in comparison with the control population who have not had that additional carcinogenic experience, if such there was.'

121

Fine, I said, but why not carry out a follow-up study of those lung-cancer deaths to see if they were smokers or not?

He said that if the study starts to show a significant increase in lung cancer among the population who went to the tests, then that is certainly something that may well have to be done.

But not in this study?

Not immediately in this study. For reasons of time, if for nothing else.

After we'd kicked around the non sequitur in the protocol that I've already described, we got back to the matter of time. How important is speed? 'Oh, speed certainly affects our considerations here. If we got into, for example, the study of genetic effects, or we got into the study of cataract, which involved going back through medical records and the medical practitioners of people involved, it would add years to the study.' He said they're hoping to get something out by the end of 1986.

I said that a cynic might say they would end up doing not what was right but what was available. Dr Dennis seemed unwounded. 'We're trying to do what is right and what is possible,' he said.

THE INFINITELY ELASTIC BLUE BOOK

I believe him. For one thing, the NRPB has a good track record in making this sort of study. (One of their clients has been Greenpeace.) For another thing, it is a huge project. The Ministry of Defence has what's called a blue book listing everyone who took part in the tests. When the protocol came out the blue book held about 12,000 names. Then the MOD looked harder and found a further 8,000. So the study has to check the health of 20,000 men and compare it with that of another 20,000 men who match them as closely as possible. The basic work of naming those 40,000 is being done by MOD researchers but the NRPB is taking 1% of the names at random and double-checking them to make sure the job is being done accurately and fairly. The health data about the 40,000 – dead or alive, sick or well – comes from the NHS Central Register. Given the data, the people at the NRPB can analyse it umpteen different ways. They are looking at what's happened to all the men who were monitored for radiation, since the MOD has supplied their records of exposure. They are looking at all the others, who were considered safe and not in need of monitoring. They are paying special attention to the small groups known to have got more radiation than usual. And so on. All these are being compared with the Control Group.

I believe Dr Dennis when he says they're trying to do what's right and what's possible. So why do I have reservations? Why this feeling that, come the end of 1986, the study will announce its findings and prove neither one thing nor the other?

It's all a matter of size and speed.

Size first. The way the MOD blue book has mushroomed in recent years – from 8,000 to 12,000 to 20,000 – is not reassuring. The hard truth is that nobody at the MOD knows exactly how many men served at the tests. When the blue book held 12,000 names they were made up of about 6,000 from the Royal Navy, 2,000 from the Army, 3,000 from the RAF and 1,000 UK civilians. That was the state of play when the protocol was published, and it was a nonsense. Three times as many sailors as soldiers? More airmen than soldiers? Absurd. How could it possibly be? The answer is to be found in the protocol, in a description of the way the blue book was compiled. Some people had been easy to find. All those who were issued with personal dosemeters were listed by the AWRE, for instance. The Ministry of Supply kept good records. (Hence all those civilians.) Ships' companies were listed in ships' ledgers. (Hence all those sailors.) But when it came to the Army: 'Possibly the members of two Army regiments and one Army construction unit which were stationed on Christmas Island for the tests.' Pretty thin pickings for the brown jobs, when you consider that the *Daily Telegraph* reported on 4 June 1957 that 4,260 men were on Christmas Island, and an item in the *Mid Pacific News* of 1958 says that at the height of operations the catering services were providing enough meals for 6,000 men a day.

Well, the MOD researchers have searched about, and now that the blue book has got up to 20,000 men the ratio between the Services has changed dramatically. Now the total is split roughly equally between the Army, Navy and RAF, which makes more sense. Perhaps I am ungrateful but I still feel dubious. Twenty thousand is a nice round figure. Too round. I suspect that, because the Army was not arranged like the Navy; because a lot of soldiers came and went – replacements, additions, temporary postings – the Army records are a lot less helpful to the MOD researchers. Therefore that round figure could well be a thousand out, or two thousand, or three. The very fact that the NRPB has identified previously unknown nuclear-test veterans when checking out names for its Control Group shows how scrupulously the study is being carried out; but it also shows how incomplete the Study Group is. And that list, of course, is absolutely fundamental to its success. If the NRPB study has found all the sailors (who were usually out at sea and relatively distant from the explosions) but not all the soldiers, then the whole thing may be lopsided from the start.

PREDICTING THE EPITAPH

The element of speed is even more important. I have no doubt that the NRPB will be fair and efficient. But they can only do what the MOD has agreed to; and seen through the MOD's eyes this is a political operation. There can be no doubt what result the Ministry hopes to hear, and hear quickly. But because of the need for speed, this has become a study into what can be found *fast*, not what *needs* to be found if the public worry that Adam Butler spoke of is to be satisfied. Cancer is not the only question; it merely happens to be the question most easily tackled. The Government has avoided the questions of genetic damage and cataract because these are difficult questions. That attitude may make for an easy life in the short term, but not in the long. Those issues simply will not

124

go away. And I honestly don't believe they are so hard to tackle as Dr Dennis suggests. If I can find 25 cases of cataracts in just a few weeks, surely the combined forces of the MOD and the NRPB wouldn't need years to finish the job? The epitaph on this MOD inquiry, I suspect, will be: All right as far as it went, but it didn't go far enough – because it had to get somewhere in a hurry.

TAILPIECE

What happened to the other 204? 796 men replied to the questionnaire, which means 204 didn't. Why?

It would be nice to know, but it would take another inquiry to find out. Mind you, a 79.6% response is not at all bad. Far from it. I worked in ad agencies long enough to know how difficult it is to get anyone to answer a letter, even if you bribe them. (We once tried scotch-taping money to the appeal, which sometimes worked but usually they just kept the money.) It takes powerful leverage to get the average bloke to write anything, let alone his medical history. Most societies or associations would be surprised and delighted to get a 79% response to a mailing. On the other hand the BNTVA is no ordinary association. You'd expect *all* its members to react with especial enthusiasm to a project like this one. So what happened to the silent 204?

Well, a few times the questionnaire bounced back, marked 'Gone Away'. So some never got it. Some got it and lost it; some got it and lost hope. Maybe a few were so sick of being sick that they didn't want to answer any more questions; maybe a few felt so thoroughly fit that they saw no point in returning a blank form. Why the others didn't answer remains a mystery.

TAILPIECE TWO

Anyone who's had enough of death, disease and deformity should skip this bit. It's a round-up of the findings of the rest of the BNTVA study.

Two things surprised me: the sheer number of men suffering from skin complaints, and the number of men with psychological problems ranging from lack of confidence to fear of thunderstorms.

THE SKIN

More than half the veterans reported some kind of skin trouble: 409 out of 796. Those with a persistent and/or severe rash totalled 170. Erythema – redness of the skin – was reported by 68 men. 95 have developed warty growths and 5 have multiple lumps on the body, bigger than warty growths. 71 suffer from cracked skin.

In many cases the rash is far worse than it sounds. One veteran described his condition:

> 'Some time after the first test I witnessed in November 1956 I developed an awful itching skin rash. I would always be scratching and making myself bleed. . . . So when I got back in UK I had to go to see a specialist at Halton Hospital, who said I had got scabies. The funny thing is I have still got them and after sleeping with my wife for 25 years she has not as yet contracted them.'
> (Scabies is a contagious skin infection.) 'I suppose miracles like that do happen, according to the government.'

However, it's no joke going through life unable to wear a short-sleeved shirt or a t-shirt, which is the daily reality for that man and other veterans. Whatever it is that has happened to their skin, exposure to any sunlight brings swift and agonising results. One veteran's holiday came to an end and he found himself in hospital, all because he took his shirt off.

Not all rashes are as serious as that, but they all need treatment. Since he left Christmas Island, Gary Collins has been permanently renewing prescriptions for creams to treat his arms and scalp. Others are luckier, having rashes that come and go, often according to the weather and the temperature.

Various theories have been suggested for this plague of skin

126

complaints. Erythema is a known result of radiation, but maybe it was caused by all that exposure to the sun. The warty growths may be linked to the boils and abscesses that so many servicemen got – blamed on the saltwater showers, or the shortage of fresh fruit and vegetables, or the bedbugs, or a combination of all three.

For every other serviceman to come home from Christmas Island with a skin complaint seems more than bad luck. It's hard to believe that the same ratio holds true for all men who served in the tropics. But whether or not it's related to the explosions is anyone's guess.

THE MIND

About one man in seven who served at the test sites has been in some kind of psychological trouble, and most still are.

Psychological trouble covers a wide range of difficulties. It means a man suffers bouts of depression (or constant depression), or he is in a state of mental confusion, or he lacks confidence to an extent that is damaging, or his memory is deteriorating. Or in some men the symptoms are more obvious. For no apparent reason they develop uncontrollable trembling, or a fear of loud noises that can turn a thunderstorm into torment, or their personality changes and they start behaving irrationally, unpredictably, with outbursts of unexplained anger.

The questionnaires are, of course, confidential. The information is tabulated. No names are published. All the same, it is remarkable that 117 men out of 796 were prepared to indicate some kind of psychological damage in their lives – not something most people are ready to concede, let alone describe. But does the fact that these cases were reported make them medically significant? It's tempting to speculate what the effect of witnessing nuclear explosions might have been on impressionable young minds. There is evidence that a few were disturbed by the experience, but only a few. It seems that the vast majority of servicemen took each day as it came (the only way to survive National Service) and emerged unscarred. One in seven is an unhappy ratio – but no higher than the proportion of all of us who, at some point in our lives, need treatment for mental illness.

THE REST OF THE BODY

Most of the other figures are unsurprising, given that the average respondent is in his late forties or early fifties. 47 men complained of stomach disorders and 49 have duodenal ulcers. 60 have heart problems. 26 repeatedly suffer from migraine or severe headaches. Many report what they consider excessive loss of hair (63), or loss of teeth (103), or loss of hearing (67). Most of all consider that their eyesight is worse than it should be (130, not counting men with cataracts). The figure for persistent diarrhoea is surprisingly high at 46, and in many cases it dates back to the nuclear tests. Diarrhoea is only funny when somebody else has it; more than one veteran's life has been ruined by it. Then there is sterility and/or impotence (they are often confused) with a total of 36. And finally, miscarriage. 121 couples suffered this misfortune, and all told, 172 miscarriages are reported.

All of these disorders or illnesses have been linked to radiation. There was, for instance, a lot of diarrhoea among the survivors at Hiroshima. Some eventually lost their hair. Others became sterile. But all you can say about the figures in the previous paragraph is that they reflect the sort of conditions you might expect to find in 796 British men whose bodies are beginning to show the strain of the years.

So the crucial findings of the BNTVA study are those covering cancers, deformities and cataracts.

There is one final figure. 113 men reported that there is nothing wrong with their health. They are fit.

On that more optimistic note, onwards to Chapter 3.

POST MORTEM

What could have gone wrong?

There are two ways of looking at that question. The first is technical. Officially the tests were quite safe because according to the scientists it was technically impossible for anyone to get hurt. So if someone did get hurt, as the veterans claim, what could science have overlooked?

The second aspect is purely human. How competent and reliable were the men in charge of the tests? Did they in fact make mistakes?

RADIATION VERSUS HEAT VERSUS BLAST, OR YOU ONLY DIE ONCE

You will have grasped by now that this is not one of those books that gives you a crash course in nuclear physics before it gets down to the meat of the argument. If you want to know the difference between uranium-235 and uranium-238 there are other people better qualified than I am to tell you. All I'm going to run through here are the inescapably relevant and important facts – what happens when a nuclear weapon explodes and in particular what happens to the radiation.

By which, of course, I mean ionizing radiation. There are other sorts – heat radiates, and light radiates, and radio signals radiate – but in this book (as in most discussions about the nuclear tests) radiation means ionizing radiation, the stuff that gives you cancer if you get too big a dose. *That* radiation.

You may be surprised to know that radiation is not the major threat to people who are near a nuclear explosion. The explosion certainly releases a colossal amount of radiation, so intense that it is lethal up to a certain radius from the point of detonation, but most people inside that radius are going to be killed by heat or blast. So most of the radiation danger is very largely of academic interest. The corpse that has been roasted or crushed cannot be killed any more thoroughly by the radiation pounding it.

Most of the energy given off by nuclear weapons is not radiation: quite the reverse. At Hiroshima and Nagasaki only about 15% of the energy of the atomic bombs went into radiation, and that proportion seems to hold good, more or less, for all nuclear weapons. The bulk of the energy goes into blast, most of what's left goes into heat, and between 15% and 20% goes into radiation.

(These three totally distinct dangers are worth remembering when you consider the comments and complaints of veterans about the ways they were or were not protected at the test sites. A common remark is: 'We were not given any protective clothing.' That statement must prompt the question: Protective against what? Against heat, or against blast, or against radiation? The man who wore cotton overalls and antiflash headgear as compared with the man who wore shorts and sandals might have been better protected against flash and heat, and perhaps even against blast, but that says nothing about protection against radiation. The best protection against radiation is six inches of concrete, not protective clothing. However, I'm getting ahead of myself. Back to the explosion.)

Different bombs release different patterns of radiation, but as far as science knows the four types that matter are alpha, beta, gamma and neutron. The damage they can do to you depends on whether they are outside you and trying to get in, or inside because you've eaten or inhaled them.

Start with the risk of external exposure at the moment of the explosion. Forget alpha and beta particles. Both have such a short range that nobody could get that close to them anyway. Gamma rays are much more penetrating and travel much further. They are steadily absorbed as they pass through the air. This rate of absorption depends upon the density of the air which in turn varies according to the height at which the explosion took place, but usually when you're considering the range of gamma rays you're talking about a maximum of two kilometres. I say 'usually' because there is a phenomenon known as hydrodynamic enhancement of gamma rays. After the shock wave from the bomb spreads out, the air density behind it is for a while abnormally low, so the later gamma rays from the explosion go through it more easily and travel further. It would be wise to reckon the range of gamma rays at double the conventional figure: 4-5 kilometres. Neutrons have even greater penetrating power than gamma rays but, like gamma rays, they become weakened and absorbed the further they travel through air. It's impossible to lay down hard and fast rules about this because the bigger the bomb, the more penetrating the radiation; however you can get an idea of how rapidly the neutron dose diminishes as the neutrons travel outwards from this example given by Joseph Rotblat. 'A gray' is a unit of radiation dose. 'Slant distance' is the distance from a given point on the surface of the Earth to the point where the explosion took place. At a slant distance of one kilometre, Rotblat says, a one-megaton thermonuclear bomb would deliver a dose of about 2,000 gray; at two kilometres the dose would be about four gray. Rotblat stresses that these calculations are for an assumed design of weapon and for a specified air density. Change the weapon (for instance to produce more neutrons) and change the air and you'd get a very different result. Nevertheless it looks as if we're talking about the same maximum range for neutrons as for gamma rays.

What this means is that the spread of direct, initial radiation (forget fallout for a minute) is such that anyone, say, six kilometres from the centre of the explosion would be relatively safe from radiation. Indeed, except for 'small' bombs (atom bombs of less than 10 kilotons, or neutron bombs) the area covered by lethal radiation is less than the area covered by lethal blast and far less than the area covered by lethal heat.

Again, Rotblat is the best source. He has calculated that a one-kiloton bomb would create areas of lethal damage of 1.5 square kilometres from blast, 1.3 square kilometres from heat, and 2.9 square kilometres from radiation. That's at the bottom of the scale: the smallest bomb. With a ten-kiloton bomb, the area of lethal damage from heat is 11.2 square kilometres – more than double the area of lethal damage from blast or from radiation. (The Hiroshima bomb, incidentally, was 13 kilotons.) And so it goes. When you get up to hydrogen bombs, the difference is enormous. When a one-megaton bomb explodes, heat creates an area of lethal damage nearly twenty times as big as that made by radiation. At ten megatons it's thirty times as big.

DIRECT, INITIAL RADIATION: A VERY POOR THIRD

The message is simple. With very small nuclear weapons, initial radiation damage reaches beyond heat and blast damage. With bigger weapons, the effects of blast and heat completely swamp the threat from initial radiation.

Of the 21 nuclear weapons that Britain exploded, all nine tests at Christmas Island, including Malden Island, were big by those terms. Seven were H-bombs and the other two were A-bombs of at least 20 kilotons. If all the men who witnessed those tests were safe from heat and blast – and although I've heard of cases of extreme discomfort, it seems that nobody needed treatment for burns and no legs or arms were broken – then they were well beyond the range of initial radiation.

With the tests in Australia it's harder to be sure. Three of the twelve are described as low-yield, meaning 1–20 kiloton. The other nine are put in the 'kiloton-yield range (1–1,000 kiloton)' but if they had been less than 20 kiloton it seems likely that the British government would have claimed credit for its moderation and called them low-yield. Certainly the three Monte Bello explosions were far from small. So nine times out of twelve, initial radiation was out-reached by the lethal range of blast or heat. To make out any kind of case for damage from initial radiation you would have to be able to show that the victim was less than five kilometres from Ground Zero. Nobody that I've talked to has claimed to have been that close, and it's generally agreed that the hydrogen bombs were exploded at least 25 miles and perhaps as much as 40 miles from the nearest observers.

If that was the case, there should have been no direct risk to the outside of the body from initial radiation – that is, radiation at the time of explosion and in the minute or minutes afterwards. As the fireball climbs, it obviously takes most of the source of radiation even further away, so the risk of contamination is further reduced.

FALLOUT IN THE LAP OF THE GODS

The next big risk is from fallout. Every nuclear weapon makes fallout. Whether or not that fallout harms anyone nearby depends on two things: the height of the burst and the direction of the wind.

If the bomb is detonated so low that the fireball touches the ground or the sea, it sucks up a huge amount of earth or water which is made highly radioactive. As the nuclear cloud cools off, this stuff starts to fall. If the winds are as predicted, the fallout will be blown into an area where there is nobody underneath to get contaminated.

Once the bomb has gone off you are in the lap of the gods and things can go wrong. The winds may not co-operate: they may blow as predicted at one height but in a very different direction at another – this happened after the second Monte Bello explosion of 1956. It might rain. If the rain meets the fallout cloud, some of the radioactive particles will get washed down as 'rain-out'. It rained at least once on Christmas Island on the day of a test.

As always, the quality of radioactivity in fallout varies according to the nature of the bomb and where it went off; in any case it's a very complex mixture. Most of the radiation is beta and gamma, but there are also some neutrons and alpha-particles emitting radiation. There are four ways this radiation can reach people. The fallout cloud emits radiation as it passes overhead, so anyone underneath might get an external dose from it. As the fallout comes to earth, anyone in that area who is unprotected might swallow or breathe in the radioactive particles. When it is lying on the ground it is releasing radiation. And finally, if it gets eaten by animals who later provide milk or meat, the radioactivity ends up inside the eater. A similar food chain applies to contaminated plants or water.

During these processes the danger from fallout varies according to the type of radiation and whether it's outside the body or inside. To oversimplify: gamma and neutron radiations can be very damaging when they strike from the outside but much less so when they are inside, neutron radiation being virtually harmless then. Alpha and beta radiations by contrast are less of a threat from the outside but far more damaging if the radioactive particles get swallowed or breathed. In this respect alpha particles are the worst.

If the fireball does *not* touch the ground or the sea, there should be the absolute minimum of fallout. Of course the bomb will be blown to bits and every particle of its casing and contents will be hugely radioactive, but all that will go upwards. The bigger the bomb, the higher it will go. It's still fallout, but if it reaches the stratosphere the winds will blow it around the globe and it will take months, maybe years to fall. Everyone in the world may get a share.

1500 TONS OF HOT DIRT

Of the 21 British tests, the 12 Australian explosions were nearly all dirty and the 9 at Christmas Island were all clean. All but three of the Australian tests were surface explosions, either at ground level (or sea level) or detonated on a tower about 100 feet above the ground. The three airbursts used aircraft or a tethered balloon. Some of the dirty bursts were dirtier than others. The very first – the 1952 obliteration of HMS *Plym* –

could hardly have been dirtier, since it turned 1,500 tons of frigate into radioactive particles. And it seems that the second 1956 Monto Bello explosion was calculated to make a big fallout cloud, since HMS *Diana* had been sent a long way there to sail through it.

All this was common knowledge. John Unwin, who was 20 when he went to Christmas Island with the Royal Engineers, told me: 'I remember well, while preparing for nuclear test duty, the verbal assurance that Operation Grapple (the Christmas Island series) was a "clean test" and I now believe this to be the case. However, the inference that pre-1957 tests were 'dirty' did not escape me.'

Apart from the possibility of rain-out on the island and on ships at sea, it's generally agreed that all the Christmas Island and Malden Island tests were clean. Detonation of the H-bomb took place high in the sky, and such radioactive debris as there was should have been transported to the stratosphere. The two A-bombs were carried by tethered balloons, high enough to keep the fireballs well away from the ground, and the mushroom clouds were blown out to sea. If all that is so, then any danger from fallout at Christmas Island virtually disappears.

However, that's not the end of the story. As well as initial radiation and radiation from fallout there is a third form of radioactivity produced by a nuclear explosion.

This is induced radioactivity. When neutrons from the initial radiation hit the sea or the ground or whatever happens to be in the immediate neighbourhood, they make that area radioactive. How radioactive depends on the height of the burst, the power of the bomb and also its design: some bombs are designed to produce neutrons in great quantity. Nevertheless, underneath a high-burst bomb there will be an area made radioactive. This induced radioactivity releases radiation which could be dangerous for a few days before it fades to next to nothing after a week or so.

* * *

WHAT COULD HAVE GONE WRONG?
THE TECHNICAL FACTOR

There are times when it seems to me that the Christmas Island story is a long fight between two blind men.

On the one side is the nuclear veteran, swinging doggedly in the hope that a big punch will connect, usually missing, often wasting his energy, and growing more desperate as time passes and no result is in sight. On the other side is the Defence Secretary, keeping his head down and his guard up, hoping the other man will wear himself out, but knowing the crowd is more and more on the veteran's side.

The veteran is convinced he's been sold down the river by the State and so he refuses to trust anyone in authority. Everything that's happened to him since the bomb – from bronchitis to dyslexia – gets blamed on the bomb. A lot of that is nonsense, but it contains a small core of truth. The veteran who has not only posterior-lens cataracts but also leukemia doesn't need to shout to make his case: the facts are loud enough. However, the MOD has no wish to listen, let alone get into any kind of debate. All it can do is stonewall. Its policy is one of stout denial, because it knows that the merest hint of an admission of official negligence would arouse not just one veteran but all twenty thousand of them. And the MOD can't afford that.

The veteran cannot see a way out, and the MOD dare not look for one. And so the fight between two blind men goes on.

To get a saner view, I went to see Joseph Rotblat at his home in West Hampstead.

BANG! OKAY, WHAT NEXT?

Professor Rotblat left Poland two days before the Germans invaded, in 1939. It wasn't a planned escape – he was simply returning to Liverpool where he was doing a year's research – but it decided his future. Hitler must be defeated. The concept of a nuclear explosion had already occurred to Rotblat (as it had to others). Eventually he found himself in Los Alamos, working with the Americans on the atom bomb.

Rotblat was a brilliant nuclear physicist and there is no question that he contributed greatly to the Manhattan project; but unlike most of his colleagues his mind reached beyond scientific curiosity (have we done our sums right? What will happen when we explode the bomb?) to the much more difficult matters of morality, of what *harm* they might all be doing. It came as a shock when, in 1944, General Groves, the head of the Manhattan project, told him: 'You realise of course that the real purpose of making the bomb is to subdue our chief enemy, the Russians.' That year, Rotblat left the project and came back to Britain.

He turned from nuclear physics to medical physics (he is Emeritus Professor of Physics at the University of London) and especially to radiation biology. Today, at the age of 77, he probably knows as much about the effects of nuclear weapons as anyone in the world. He was a founder of the Pugwash Conference – a permanent attempt by scientists to bring peace to the world – and is still active in its efforts. When I saw him he had recently returned from a month of conferences in Europe, Japan and South America. Professor Rotblat is in retirement now, though you could have fooled me.

OUT OF DEADLOCK

We began by talking about the fundamental, head-banging incompatibility of the two sides. *Apparent* incompatibility. Professor Rotblat takes them both seriously. He does not dismiss the assurances of the MOD and the AWRE: the scientists on Christmas Island were not fools. He is equally impressed by the medical histories of veterans which indicate an excess of cancers, especially blood cancers, leukemias, and also a significant proportion of service people who have contracted cataracts in an age group where one would not expect to see cataracts – especially when these cataracts are moreover of a type not normally found among aged people.

'I was trying to assume that both sides are correct,' he told me, 'to see if it is possible to find a reason for this discrepancy. Therefore I was looking for some possible sources of exposure which would *not* have been recorded on the monitors.' And he added that many people were not monitored at all, so there's no means of saying whether they were exposed to radiation or not. All we have is the MOD's assurance that they were a safe distance from the explosions.

At this point he backtracked a little to say something more about cataracts. 'It is generally assumed that in order to produce cataracts one needs much higher doses of radiation than to produce cancer, because for cancer there is no threshold: any increase in the amount of radiation is likely to increase the probability of cancer. For cataracts it's assumed that one needs at least over a hundred rads – units of radiation – to produce cataract.'

(That is a lot of rads. A rad is very roughly equivalent to a roentgen. To give an idea: the aircrew flying cloud-sampling operations during a test in Australia are reported to have been exposed to 24.5 roentgens.)

THE WAY IT REALLY WAS

'Now, I look at the disposition of the service people on the map of Christmas Island; I look at the place where the explosions occurred; I studied the direction of the wind, and also I notice a number of people saying that rain came down soon after the explosion. Generally one would not have expected any fallout to occur because the bombs were exploded at such a height that it should not have produced any fallout. However we know now that there is a phenomenon called rain-out. Rain-out means that some of the radioactive materials which are produced in the explosion, which normally would be sucked up and go very high into the stratosphere, that sometimes they encounter a condensation cloud.'

(It may seem strange that a fireball and a condensation cloud can co-exist, but a nuclear explosion is a highly complex series

138

of events. When AWRE made a film of Christmas Island tests, the commentary included this statement: 'As it rises the fireball begins to assume a doughnut shape. Atmosphere is very moist and condensation occurs. This condensation is apparent in the remarkable white spike rising towards the mushroom stem.')

Given a condensation cloud, Professor Rotblat went on, 'particles may condense on this and then the condensation cloud would come down as rain which has now a certain amount of radioactivity.

'Of course we can say there was no cloud, there was a blue sky. It turns out now – this again I have learned recently – that the rain-out could be self-induced: that the actual up-draught of the hot air which is produced inside the fire, that this may result in the clouds being formed. And this may scavenge some of the radioactive particles.

'We know this happened at Hiroshima and Nagasaki, because there too the height of the explosion was such as not to produce fallout. Moreover the skies were blue – the condition for using, for dropping the bomb was it should be clear, blue sky. And yet in both cases, about half an hour after the explosion rain was reported. This rain, called "black rain", came down and it contained some radioactive materials.'

(The air around Christmas Island is fairly humid. The island has an average annual rainfall of 34 inches, an average relative humidity of 70%, and an average cloud cover of one-half. The sky *above* the island is usually clear but there are plenty of clouds *around* it.)

The evidence of letters from servicemen who experienced rainfall at the time of a test – in particular sailors on HMS *Narvik* who said it 'absolutely bucketed down' while an H-bomb cloud was overhead – impressed Professor Rotblat. Should it rain on Christmas Island, he said, most of it will go into the lagoon. (The place is actually half land and half lagoon.) It will take some time before the rain-out is diluted.

'Now, if people bathe and swim, they are likely to swallow a certain amount of water. It's inevitable, almost. Therefore if this water was contaminated by radioactivity, this might have given rise to *internal* exposure.' Internal exposure didn't register on the external monitors worn by servicemen – which in any case would not have reacted to the type of radioactivity we're talking about. 'And this gave me the idea of the mechanism with which service people might have been exposed to radiation even though nobody had expected it before.'

Interesting. But some servicemen couldn't swim and others (as we know from interviews) simply didn't have time to swim. What of them?

'Another way would be washing. I think fresh water was very hard to come by there, they had to use the water from the lagoon.' (This is so. All water for what the Services call ablutions came from the lagoon. Showering and tooth-cleaning was done with lagoon water.) 'The other factor might be, of course, eating fish, because if any radioactivity did come down into the water, the fish no doubt could have swallowed it and then become radioactive.' And he described the sequence: very fine particles of radioactive material are taken up by plankton, small fish eat the plankton, they in turn are eaten by larger fish and so the process goes on, with the material being concentrated at each stage until in some cases it could be hundreds of times greater than the original concentration in the water.

Which reminded me of the story Major James Carman told on 'Panorama' in 1983, about a celebration dinner on Christmas Island. Crayfish featured on the menu. Although the background reading was nil, a geiger counter got a strong reading from the crayfish; and when an RAF officer ate some, with a geiger counter held in his outstretched hand (to keep it remote from the crayfish), the counter began clicking after a couple of minutes – presumably the time it took for the radioactivity from the crayfish to circulate through his system.

'Such fish are eaten,' Professor Rotblat said, 'and of course one could take in a much larger amount of radioactivity than would normally be expected by drinking the water direct.'

Certainly, great quantities of fish were caught. Wally Jackson remembered:

'Shark, red snapper, mullet. Mullet — we used to catch mullet, just threw a bare hook in, into the shoal of mullet and you could catch 'em just like that. It was a case of as soon as the hook hit the water. . . . We used to throw a bucket of gash in, y'see, these mullet used to come around a bucket of gash and then you'd throw a hook in, into the gash itself, like, y'know — they'd just snap it up. There was that many of them going for food. . . . And within 3 or 4 minutes you could have enough fish to feed the ship's company for the day, like.'

In addition to serving the regular menu, Ken Taylor, a Navy cook stationed on the island, got permission to sell fish-and-chips. The fish was often tuna and swordfish:

'They sent out a motor fishingboat and they used to bring it in like about 4 o'clock in the afternoon, and we would skin it and bone it ready for in the evening like. Because it wasn't as a meal as such. It was like a private fish shop, sort of business.'

If the water, or the fish in the water, was contaminated it would have been with alpha particles or beta particles. Once inside the human body these materials enter the bloodstream and by that means reach the various organs. 'There, of course,' Professor Rotblat said, 'they could act in a way that will eventually produce either cancer or cataract.'

The most dangerous form of radioactivity is plutonium, which emits alpha particles. Plutonium was used as the trigger for the seven H-bombs exploded at Christmas and Malden Islands. Plutonium is the most poisonous substance in the world, and there is no particle of it so small that it cannot do you harm if it gets inside you. Moreover, it doesn't fade away

141

in a few days or months, like a lot of radioactivity. Plutonium-239 has a half-life of 24,400 years, which means it takes that long for the stuff to decay to half its strength.

RAIN-OUT OF RADIOACTIVITY

So. According to Joseph Rotblat's hypothesis, there was rain-out at Christmas Island, there could have been self-induced rain-out which means that each and every explosion might have caused some rain-out, and the scavenging action of these rain-outs could have carried radioactive particles into the sea where this radioactivity would have become greatly intensified as it passed through the food chain until it was taken in by servicemen eating fish. And even if they were wearing monitors (which most were not) this internal contamination would not have been detected. The same applies to any intake from swimming or washing in lagoon water.

It's a hypothesis. It still needs to be proved by a statistical study. But then, almost *everything* about low-level radiation still needs to be proved. What most scientists believed they knew for sure now turns out to be very uncertain.

'I would say that despite all the research done over so many years,' Joseph Rotblat told me, 'we still do not know how to calculate the increased probability of cancer being induced by very small doses of radiation, from different types of radiation. In fact if anything we are now more confused than we were before.'

WASHOUT OF KNOWLEDGE

The trouble is that everyone has relied on the data from Hiroshima and Nagasaki, because, let's face it: what other real evidence is there? The most detailed studies were made, the different radiation doses at the two cities were carefully calculated, and the conclusion was that Nagasaki got virtually nothing but gamma-ray radiation while at Hiroshima it was mainly neutron radiation. On the strength of that it was confidently deduced that a low dose of neutrons is far more likely to produce cancer than a low dose of gamma rays.

'Now all this has been turned upside-down,' Professor Rotblat said. 'New studies have been made – by a laboratory you don't expect to cause alarm among people, namely the Livermore Laboratory.' (This is the Lawrence Livermore National Laboratory in California, where they spend their time designing new nuclear weapons.) 'They pointed out that the dosimetry, the way of measuring the radiation doses at these two Japanese cities, was all wrong! And that there were practically no neutrons in either of the cities, that all of the effects were gamma rays.'

Back to square one, almost. The physical side of it has to be re-evaluated, and then the biological side.

'Therefore at the present moment we know even less about the induction of tumours by radiation than we knew before. All the indications are, from the preliminary measurements, that the probability of inducing cancer by radiation will go up for gamma rays, but for neutrons we don't know anything at all. This is a very sad story, that the more we study the less we know. It would be wise to keep an open mind.'

*   *   *

THE GREAT DETECTIVE MISSES A FEW CLUES

'There is no evidence that this form of cancer would be induced by exposure to ionising radiation and the film badge which Sapper Duggan wore, in common with all those liable to be exposed to radiation, gives no record of exposure. I think we can take it, therefore, that Sapper Duggan did not die as the result of his service on Christmas Island.'

– Fred Mulley, Deputy Secretary of State for Defence, to the Rt Hon. Harold Wilson, MP, on 18 June 1965.

That is the standard MOD response to claims from Christmas Island widows. I've read so many letters like that, with minor variations, that I feel sure the Ministry has the original on a word processor. On the face of it, the argument is hard to beat: if the man was monitored for radiation and the monitor found none, what is left to discuss?

For a start, the monitors are worth discussing. Some worked well, some didn't work well, and even the best were useless if nobody looked at them, which also happened.

UNDERRATING THE GONADS BY 40%

In 1957, C. F. Barnaby of AWRE wrote a report with the intriguing title: *The Dose Received at Various Parts of the Body by a Man Walking over Contaminated Ground.* Too bad: the man turned out not to be a man but a hermaphrodite and he/she walked nowhere, because it was made of wood. Mr Barnaby had indulged in a little literary licence.

In 1956, at Maralinga, AWRE built a standard man from mahogany, 5 ft 11 in. tall, 160 lbs, and drilled holes in various crucial places – base of lung, spleen, intestine, testicles and ovaries. They plugged the holes with dosimeters, dressed the dummy in standard protective clothing – underwear, boiler-suit, socks, boots, gloves and gas mask – and put it in a contaminated area where it would get a known dose of radiation. Presumably the dummy also wore a film badge, although the report doesn't actually say so.

Men working in contaminated areas were usually monitored with a film badge or a quartz-fibre dosimeter, which looked like a pen. Both were usually worn at chest level. The purpose of this experiment was to compare the doses received by the vital organs of the dummy with the doses recorded on the monitors. The conclusions are worth printing in full:

'It seems from these results that the film badge records the dose to the organs in the upper half of the body satisfactorily but that the intestine and testicles receive about 40% more dose than that recorded on the dosimeters normally worn. A difference between the readings of the PM1 film and the dosimeter is commonly found. It is usual to consider the film reading as being more accurate and use the dosimeter as a check, if necessary.'

So on that occasion, dosimeter readings below the waist were too low by 40%. True, AWRE claimed they paid more attention to film-badge readings. But film badges were not usually worn below the waist – and what's more, film-badge readings were not always totally dependable. During the London hearings of the Australian Royal Commission on British nuclear tests, Mr W. G. McDougall was questioned about a report he had written at Maralinga on monitoring procedures. This report revealed that, in the forward area, sometimes the dosimeters and the film badges agreed and sometimes the film dose was double what the dosimeters recorded; however at the airfield it was sometimes the reverse: film doses were only *half* the dosimeter doses being recorded for ground crew.

Mark Mildred represented the British Nuclear Tests Veterans Association at the hearings.

> *Mark Mildred*: Was your confidence at all shaken by the rather startling news that readings between film badge and dosimeter could vary between 2 to 1 and 1 to 2?
>
> *Mr McDougall*: Not particularly. I would put much more confidence in the film badge in those days. I think we did suspect the dosimeters to some extent, depending on the type of radiation. The difference is not of an enormous order. If it had been of the order of 10 to 1, one would have been shaken. Of the order of 2 to 1 with accuracy with which we work it was reasonable.

CARRY ON REGARDLESS

The implication is that the doses of radiation being received were so small that you could double the reading, quadruple it, and the man still wouldn't be in danger. As a generalisation that might well have a lot of truth in it. But with thousands of men doing very different jobs all over the place, there were bound to be exceptions. Take Michael Hardisty's experience. He was an RAF engine mechanic with 76 Squadron, first on Operation Antler in Australia and then on Grapple X on Christmas Island. In his statement to the Australian Royal Commission he said:

> 'When working on aircraft which had been cloud-sampling we were issued with protective clothing. It was impossible to work on small 2BA nuts etc. wearing gloves. We were told to work without gloves, as there was no real danger.'

In theory, regular monitoring should have proved that point, one way or the other. The monitor used by engine mechanics looked something like a hot-air hand-dryer: you put your hands inside it, pressed a bar, and a needle swung to 'Safe' or 'Danger'. At 'Danger' a bell rang. However, in Michael Hardisty's case:

> 'The monitor machine in the hangar always went to danger when we tested ourselves after working. . . . We were told the machine was probably defective.'

Not that it seemed to matter. Interviewed by 'Panorama' Michael Hardisty said: '. . . and when new people came out and we were showing them how to do it, we would just walk up to it and put our hands in and say, "When it's clean it's like this and when there's danger the bell will ring", and the bell would start ringing and they'd look at us . . .'

Clearly, the attitude was pretty slap-happy – and not only on the part of the servicemen. That hangar monitor was not a good advertisement for the health physics teams. Their performance seems to have been patchy: sometimes strict, other times casual. Sydney Fletcher served on HMS *Campania* at Monte Bello in 1952. In his statement to the Australian Royal Commission he said:

> 'When I went ashore I was issued with a roentgen meter. I was told to look for a certain reading, and if it occurred to

leave the area quick. In common with the rest of my mates I never bothered to look, because I did not understand how it worked and nobody else bothered with them.'

Fred Dent, an engine mechanic in the RAF, was at Maralinga airfield for all four Operation Buffalo explosions in 1956. His statement said:

'Before the tests began we were all issued with a plastic film badge to record any radiation to which we were exposed. We wrote our names on these badges and during the tests the first badge with which we were issued was collected from us and we were issued with a second one. This one was never taken from us for checking, and I threw mine away into a dustbin over a year later, when packing my kit prior to flying back to England. I also took away with me my range pass, which should have been handed in on leaving but which was never collected from me.'

He was not alone. Robert Southwell was a civilian worker at the Maralinga site, often close to the forward area. His statement said:

'Most of the time we went around barechested, and the film badge with which we were issued was pinned on our shorts. I don't remember ever handing such a badge in. I know that I brought one home, and left it at my brother's house for years.'

Brian Gillman, a Sapper on Malden and Christmas Islands, brought his film badge home and gave it to his mother. Michael Hardisty says: 'My film monitor badge was never collected from me, and is still in my possession.'

Why didn't the servicemen take monitoring more seriously? One reason is the attitude of some of the decontamination units. Colin Campbell, who was an RAF driver at Maralinga, remembers a unit who 'used to tease the men sometimes by holding up a fluorescent watch near the (geiger) counter and making it sound off, and then insisting that the personnel went through the showers again.' Another reason was the suspicion that sometimes film badges were worn for purely cosmetic purposes. This emerged during an inquest into the death of a man who had served on HMS *Warrior* when he was at Malden Island for the three H-bomb tests. Raymond Knock had been a petty officer on *Warrior* and when giving evidence he was sceptical of the value of the film badges that he and everyone else wore, because they couldn't be tested on *Warrior*. The only testing facility was on board *Narvik*. 'For everything to work properly,' he said, 'these cells (film badges) should have been tested after each blast. But they weren't. We kept the same one and handed it in at the end.'

RISKY BUSINESS

Dr D. G. Stevenson, one of the few men in the world to have a Ph.D. in Laundry Studies, was involved (with AWRE) in almost all the decontamination processes for all the tests in Australia. He described the world in 1956 as being in a 'semi-emergency'.

Mark Mildred: Going back to paragraph 32 of your statement, 'risks beyond those of normal peacetime would be accepted'. Now, can you make it quite clear, did you think that in the mind of the ordinary serviceman at the tests, firstly there was any sense of semi-emergency? Were they aware of the drama of the hour or not?

Dr Stevenson: I think as far as aircrews' officers, that would have been their attitude. I think that perhaps comes out in Air Commodore Wilson's statements; and the fact –

Mark Mildred: He was not an ordinary serviceman, was he?

Dr Stevenson: I think as far as the other ranks are concerned there was no assumption or presumption that they would be exposed to risks. I think the higher risks were, as I understand, more on a volunteer basis by the aircraft. Obviously, flying through a cloud involved the risk of radiation levels above the normal accepted limits.

Mark Mildred: So far as the ordinary servicemen were concerned it was normal peacetime, was it?

Dr Stevenson: I think as far as the ordinary servicemen were concerned, the situation was very parallel to industrial workers in atomic energy establishments.

Mark Mildred: Perhaps with one difference: doesn't the word 'accepted risk' predicate knowledge of what it is that one is accepting?

Dr Stevenson: Not necessarily.

Mark Mildred: You can accept a risk without knowing what it is, can you?

Dr Stevenson: I think it depends how far you explain it, and obviously this depends on the intellect of the individual; he may be able to comprehend the risk; but to draw a parallel with industrial workers recruited to atomic energy establishments, they are instructed in procedures; they do not have to know all the details of the effects of radiation on human tissue.

Mark Mildred: So really that first sentence, rather provocative on the face of it, only applies to the top brass, does it?

Dr Stevenson: I think so, yes.

*   *   *

WHAT COULD HAVE GONE WRONG? THE HUMAN FACTOR

Bernard Perkins in a statement to the Australian Royal Commission into the British nuclear tests in Australia, about the second explosion (Mosaic 2) at Monte Bello in 1956, when he served on the command ship, HMS *Narvik*:

'I was not on duty when the explosion took place and I watched it from the deck. I went on duty at 4 p.m. This time I was sending press releases from the journalists who

149

were on board. Suddenly a signal came in direct from Sydney. It was written down on a pad, in manuscript by the operator who took it. It was from the Australian prime minister to the prime minister of Great Britain. It simply said: "What the bloody hell is going on, the cloud is drifting over the mainland?" It was a very short message and everybody stood there looking at it. The pad was on the table and we were all reading it. We were very quiet, because the captain and the scientists had been asked down to look at it. All signals received, including this one, were put onto a log. The message was sent on by the chief telegraphist in code to the UK via Singapore.'

Mr McClellan was Counsel for the Royal Commission. Lord Penney was Director of the Atomic Weapons Research Establishment from 1953 to 1959.

> *Mr McClellan*: Was there any concern – I appreciate you were not present – back at headquarters expressed to you about the Mosaic 2 cloud?
> *Lord Penney*: Again not to my knowledge.
> *Mr McClellan*: If there had been an exchange of telegrams between Prime Ministers you would have expected to know about it, would you not?
> *Lord Penney*: Certainly I would, yes.
> *Mr McClellan*: And if it is that there was an exchange and you were not told, can you offer me any explanation as to why that should be?
> *Lord Penney*: No, I cannot. I think if it happened I should have been informed and if it happened I think I would have remembered it.

Vice Admiral Sir Hugh Martell was operational commander for Mosaic.

> *Mr McClellan*: Do you recall that telegram being sent and received at that time?
> *Vice Admiral Martell*: Well, the language referred to in

that telegram was not in keeping with my scanty knowledge of Mr Menzies.

    Mr McClellan: But what about your knowledge of the
telegram?

    Vice Admiral Martell: Nothing. I was aware of the fact
some telegram had been sent and a suitable reply had been
sent back but what I cannot tell you. These things were
not addressed to *Narvik* in any way.

So – there you have it. You pays your money and you takes
your choice. Either (a) there *was* a telegram (Bernard Perkins)
or (b) if there had been a telegram I would have known and I
didn't know so there couldn't have been one (Lord Penney) or
(c) I knew nothing about the telegram (Vice Admiral Sir Hugh
Martell) or (d) I knew there was a telegram but I don't know
what was in it (Vice Admiral Sir Hugh Martell).

'YOU MAY LIVE TO REGRET THAT'

The exchanges encapsulate something of the frustrations of
the Australian Royal Commission's hearings in London. Inevitably many of the witnesses were old men trying to remember what happened thirty-plus years ago, and failing, or
becoming confused or sometimes getting short-tempered and
impatient. A certain amount of point-scoring crept into the
proceedings. Lord Penney was not in the best of health and
towards the end of his giving evidence nobody was allowed to
forget it. On the other side, counsel went through the mountains of documents with all the dedication of theologians at
work on the Dead Sea Scrolls. There was profit to be got from a
sentence, a phrase, sometimes a word. A hint of ambiguity or
the suggestion of an admission was enough to provoke long
and intense scrutiny. Many nits got picked. For all this the
British government was partly to blame. It never made much of
an effort to hide the feeling that the Commission was a waste
of time and its coming to London was a tiresome bore. Two
weeks before the hearings opened the relevant Minister, Adam

Butler, said in the House of Commons that he had studied the matter as closely as he could, and from the evidence he believed that precautions were adequate and observed. The President of the Commission, Mr J. R. McClelland (not to be confused with the Commission's counsel, Peter McClellan without a final 'd') is a forthright Australian judge. No doubt he can take Adam Butler or leave him alone. What annoyed Mr McClelland was the way the British government kept promising its full support but failing to cough up its secrets. Some observers say that the government seemed to be doling out these documents grudgingly and sluggishly; others said there was nothing special about that, it was just the way British governments always behaved. After a while things got better but by then the damage had been done. The Commission's lawyers had reacted by squeezing the last drop of juice out of everything they could find.

Not that it always took much effort. Statements by ex-servicemen made it clear that several aspects of the tests in Australia could have been handled better.

Sydney Fletcher served on board HMS *Campania*. In his statements to the Commission he recalled the voyage to Monte Bello in 1952:

> 'We had a briefing on the voyage about the bomb from the scientists. They told us quite frankly that they didn't have a clue exactly what would happen, and they could not say what would happen to future generations. As a result of this one person tried to get off his duty. We had lectures each day for a couple of weeks.'

Reginald Garbett was one of the crew of HMS *Tracker* at Monte Bello in 1952:

> 'Anyone going ashore had to wear protective clothing – overalls, wellington boots and antiflash gear. When they came back from ashore to HMS *Tracker*, I along with other crew members of HMS *Tracker* were then responsible for destroying this clothing that had been worn

ashore. None of us performing this operation of handling and destroying the clothing were given any protective equipment to carry out this operation.'

Jack Kearney also served on *Tracker*, which was the health ship for Operation Hurricane – the exploding of an atomic bomb inside HMS *Plym* in the lagoon at Monte Bello. In a letter written in 1983 he described his experience:

'About 3 weeks after the explosion I was sent for and told I would have to go into the lagoon as one of our LCM's had sank, and I was the only diver in the Fleet. On doing the dives I had a mishap and swallowed some of the sea water. On arriving back on board I left my overall hanging on some davits. Three days after the dives, the health centre sent for me and asked if the overalls on the table were mine as they were red hot. I told them about the dives I had done, one of the boffins then came with me and found that everything I had used on the dives was red hot, unfortunately for me I did not mention that I had swallowed some of the radioactive water. About 4 weeks after, on our way home I started having pains in my stomach which I had continually until arriving home in February 1953. I told the doctor on board; he laughed and said "Do you think you have an atomic stomach?"'

The question is pretty typical of the facetious way in which radiation was treated by doctors then. Whether or not Jack Kearney had an atomic stomach, the ship in which he came home – HMS *Tracker* – was radioactive in many places. A confidential report lists her condition four weeks after the explosion. Five landingcraft were still contaminated; floorboards and cordage had been jettisoned; the craft must be kept well painted to contain the radiation. Some of this was to be expected. What took the Admiralty by surprise was the way 'small local concentrations of radio-active contamination were built up in such places as under water inlets, condensers, evaporators, cable lockers etc.' *Tracker* would be contaminated for many months. However, *Tracker*'s problems were as nothing compared to the state HMS *Campania* was in. This converted aircraft carrier was supposed to come home and refit on the Clyde. That was cancelled in an order dated 22 December 1952. Scribbled on the top is the comment: 'The risk from radioactive contamination will be considerably reduced by October 1953'. Meanwhile no dockyard would have her. She lay at sea, off Sheerness, for a long time, cooling off.

* * *

Graham Mabbutt was an acting petty officer on board HMS *Zeebrugge* in 1952. In his statement to the Commission he described what happened after the Monte Bello test:

'HMS *Zeebrugge* returned to Freemantle. En route to Freemantle we had to throw the drums full of the waste materials from the sampling of radioactive matter, overboard. I was told we were going to a particularly deep part of the ocean to do this. The waste matter was in steel drums. I was in charge of winching the drums out of the tank space from the laboratory onto the upper deck and then overboard. There were 20 to 30 drums in all, and to my certain knowledge 6 to 8 of them were seeping badly. There was a problem in that the davit would not swing properly because it was too small, and the drum would catch in the scuppers. I then had to step forward and manually shove the drum clear of the ship's side. I did this because I was in charge of the operation. I remember getting splashed over the arms and legs by the seeping liquids from these drums.

'I can clearly remember a scientist who was observing these operations saying, when he saw me being splashed, "One day you may live to regret that." This raised a laugh among the ratings present as it was taken to mean that it might affect my ability to have children. Some of the drums were leaking so badly that the liquid was draining into the scuppers. There was always a scientist present

154

when the drums went overboard, but when he observed the leaking he simply shrugged his shoulders. A number of the drums, 2 or 3, failed to sink, and again the scientist shrugged his shoulders. While this operation went on we were bare-armed, with sleeves rolled up. I'm not certain what sort of trousers we were wearing but it may have been shorts.'

At most of the British nuclear test sites in Australia it was not so easy to toss the contaminated waste into the sea. Just as Monte Bello was chosen because the cluster of islands is ninety miles off the coast of West Australia, so Emu Field and Maralinga were chosen because they are in the middle of the most godforsaken wastes of Southern Australia. Very few British soldiers or airmen who got posted there were volunteers; they just 'got sent'. Dennis Tilling served with the RAF at Maralinga. He was an aircraft handler; in particular he handled Canberras on return from cloud-sampling operations. In his statement he said:

'There was no explanation at all by the authorities about the effects of radiation. Amongst the servicemen it was considered funny rather than serious if somebody became contaminated. Few of us would have had any idea of the after-effects of contamination.'

Colin Campbell was a regular in the RAF when he was posted to Australia in 1956 aged 22. He served at Maralinga Field as an MT driver. In his statement to the Commission he described an occasion when he drove a fuel bowser:

'A Canberra aircraft which had flown through the atomic cloud landed to refuel. I drove the bowser out to it and an aircraft handler connected the open-line fuel supply to the aircraft.'

Mr Campbell noticed that this man was wearing denim overalls, no gloves and no head covering.

155

'I parked the bowser between 10–15 feet of the aircraft.
... While I was doing this I saw a man with a long probe,
which he inserted into the sampling pod on the starboard
wingtip and pulled out the filter, which he put into a box.
He was wearing the same as me. I know this because if
he'd been wearing different, protective clothing and I was
not, I would have wondered why.'

Maralinga was no picnic. Anthony Brogan was a Cook's
Assistant with the RAF and witnessed four explosions – the
Operation Buffalo series of 1956. He recalls:

'Most people were moved right out of the area in case of
an accident. But we were told to stay to prepare food for
the men when they returned. Conditions were rotten. I
remember after one explosion there was a big windstorm
and there was red dust on and in everything, even the
spuds we cooked were full of it but it was still served up.'

HESELTINE LIFTS THE LID

Until 1983, the red dust in the spuds at Maralinga was an
official secret, like everything else in the Army, Navy or RAF.
Anthony Brogan would have been liable for prosecution if he
had said or written anything about it (after all, who knows
what that dust really was?) and this book would have been
impossible. The Official Secrets Act bans ex-servicemen from
revealing anything about their Service experience to anybody.
Okay, that hasn't stopped Spike Milligan writing books about
his war, but it would be enough to worry a lot of Christmas
Island veterans who feel they have enough problems without
the Special Branch knocking on the door and frightening the
children. (And not only the veterans. One of the BNTVA's
medical questionnaires was returned with a note from the
man's widow saying: 'Sorry I have been so long in answering
your letter. You will appreciate my reluctance in view of what I
thought of the Official Secrets Act. Now I know it doesn't
concern me ...' Her husband died in 1975.) So when the

Defence Secretary, Michael Heseltine, wrote to Labour's defence spokesman, John Silkin, in May 1983, his letter changed everything. 'I have no wish to inhibit the discussion of events during the British nuclear tests in Australia and the Christmas and Malden Islands,' he said, and announced that the experiences of the nuclear veterans were no longer covered by the Official Secrets Act. The only information they must not reveal is the design, construction or performance of nuclear weapons: that's still classified. But 'they would be free to talk about the general tasks they were called on to perform, the extent to which safety precautions were enforced and observed, and their own concerns for health and safety.'

It seems like a generous gesture, but as Quentin Crisp once remarked: 'The art of politics is the ability to make the inevitable seem like a matter of wise human choice.' The Defence Secretary was simply anticipating the inevitable. The veterans' association had just been formed. It had a lot of public sympathy. If the government tried to use the Official Secrets Act to gag debate about what happened on Christmas Island, that would have made it look as if there was something very nasty to hide. Since he couldn't use the Act, Mr Heseltine very intelligently collected what credit he could by *not* using it.

OFFICER I/C COCK-UPS

Shortly before the Australian Royal Commission began its hearings in London, former Flight Lieutenant Frederick Smith of No. 24 (Commonwealth) Squadron, RAF, submitted a statement to the air attaché at Australia House. In 1956 his squadron had been based at RAAF Edinborough Field in South Australia for Operation Buffalo.

> 'On one particular test, an air drop onto a mock-up village containing all the military ordnance, aircraft, animals and such, it was our duty to fly civil dignitaries, professors, medical experts etc. to view the test and give an air-view of the devastation as soon as possible after the detonation.

'However, when returning to Edinborough after the viewing, the officer in charge of the tests who was on board came up to the flight deck and said "as the majority of these people (the pax) live in Adelaide, go straight there". We duly proceeded to Adelaide civil airport and deplaned all the passengers.

'We then returned to Edinborough Field, where, to our consternation we were ordered to taxi to a remote part of the airfield and await de-contamination.

'We tried to point out that we had already landed at Adelaide Civil and deplaned our pax, but regardless the aircraft was sealed with the crew still inside and de-contaminated, a lengthy process carried out by gents garbed in what I can only describe as "space suits". The fact we had already landed at Adelaide was never mentioned again.'

In his statement Frederick Smith added: 'I gather the UK MOD insists that every precaution was taken – it is my view that precautions were totally inadequate – not through deliberate negligence but ignorance of the effects at the time.' Certainly the actions of the 'officer in charge' make no sense. Either all the passengers and crew should have been decontaminated, or none.

Officers in charge were prone to human error, as Terence Taylor, a former RAF driver/mechanic, disclosed in his statement. He too had been stationed at RAAF Edinborough Field for the Buffalo tests:

'Sometime after our arrival we were asked if we would like to see the night blast at Maralinga. Our names were put into a hat and mine was one of those pulled out. We flew from Edinborough Field to Maralinga airfield in a Hastings. When we disembarked – the Hastings was full of people from Edinborough Field – we were told by an officer to assemble over on the airfield. He explained to us, after we had assembled, that he would begin the

158

countdown, and when he reached ten, we should turn round, close our eyes, and cover them with our hands. We were all standing facing the blast, and when the officer got to seventeen, the explosion happened. There was an absolutely blinding flash. I placed my hands over my eyes and turned away. I thought, "Bloody hell, am I blinded?" We had been told that the night-time glare would be much brighter than daytime, and that it could blind us. Immediately after the explosion had finished we went back to the aircraft and flew back to Edinborough Field.'

Any other officer who had charge of men in similar circumstances would have made them turn their backs *before* he began the countdown. This officer evidently had great faith in his arithmetic and his stopwatch. In the interests of radiation medicine I can reveal that Mr Taylor was not blinded. Disillusioned, perhaps, but not blinded.

MIGHTIER YET AND MIGHTY

The biggest nuclear blast in Australia was the last: Mosaic 2, 19 June 1956. It was not the ideal time of year.

As Robert Malcomson has suggested, HMS *Diana* sailed halfway round the world to Monte Bello to test her anti-fallout system but when the first bomb was exploded she failed to rendezvous with the fallout cloud. (Mosaic 1, 16 May 1956.) The wind was not helpful. The mushroom from Mosaic 1 eventually divided, part was blown eastward and actually crossed the Australian coast – although by then, so the safety committee said, it had shed all its fallout.

There was no official suggestion that Mosaic 2 was going to be any bigger than Mosaic 1 (which had rattled a few windows on the mainland) but when it happened there was no doubt in the minds of the observers. The fireball was bigger, at least twice the size of the Mosaic 1 fireball, and it climbed a lot faster. The bang when it came was a colossal double crack that was heard two hundred miles away, deep inside Western

Australia. Given all that, it seems absurd for the British and Australian governments even to pretend that this was just another test like all the rest. But as late as 1983 the official line was that none of the tests in Australia, including Mosaic 2, was much above 20 kilotons. Then in 1984 the British government very quietly put on the shelves of the House of Lords library a document that reported Mosaic 2 to have been a 60 kiloton bomb. In 1985 the MOD released another document to the Royal Commission which said that, according to a different measuring technique, Mosaic 2 was 98 kilotons. (Mosaic 1 is listed at 16 kilotons.)

This kind of behaviour makes it extraordinarily difficult to reckon whether or not men were placed at risk. If the MOD says that an explosion was 20 kilotons, then one set of dangers applies. Increase the explosive yield fivefold and everything changes. Down through the years the MOD has gone on repeating the same stonewalling defence whenever a nuclear veteran has tried to make a claim. This defence moves in two simple stages. (1) Our records show you were never in any danger. (2) If you believe otherwise, prove it.

Yet as long as the MOD refuses to make available the most crucial pieces of evidence – the power and make-up of each bomb – it can never lose. (Do I hear the words, 'Yes, Minister!'?) The tests all took place 30 years ago. As Mr McClelland said, 'Secrecy, in the national interest, has always been a convenient alibi for failure of disclosure. But today it is hard to believe that Britain is in possession of any atomic secrets unknown to the great Nuclear Powers.'

IN HARM'S WAY

In 1953 the Chiefs of Staff were advised that the Navy needed to know what effect an atomic explosion would have on ships, their contents and equipment. That was why HMS *Diana* was at Monte Bello three years later. She had been fitted out with a makeshift sprinkler system and crude air filters, and now the Navy wanted to know how much radioactivity these would keep out. When she went into the fallout most of the crew were confined to the interior of the ship, which was conned (controlled) from below. However, some seamen were on deck, and two of them gave statements to the Commission.

Keith Syder was on deck because *Diana* was towing a whaler, filled with scientific equipment, astern and a side-running paravane. He had to attend to the hawsers, making sure they did not foul. His statement says:

'I was wearing a roentgen meter and a radiation film badge all the time I was on deck. . . . We were wearing battledress, that is, blue denim shirt and blue jeans; we were given a set of sea boots, a white heavy cotton hat, a light overall made of cotton or plastic, and I think we may have had a mask over our faces.

'Almost immediately after the explosion we began sailing towards the cloud, which was very obvious and seemed to be descending towards the sea. It was thousands of feet high and climbed for probably an hour and a half before it began to descend. We had to wait until the fallout cloud was visible before we began sailing straight into it. The cloud seemed to be made up of fine brown dust particles. The cloud was browner than fog and not so thick. The sunlight was dispersed or refracted through the cloud. When we sailed through the cloud to its far perimeter, we went about and came back through it again.'

Howard Coles was also on deck. In his statement he said:

'An arrangement of punctured firehoses was to spray water over much of the ship whilst running through radioactive fallout from a low-level atomic explosion. To evaluate the effectiveness of the system, it required that levels of radiation should be monitored while the ship was engaged in the test, only a few hours after the second Mosaic detonation. On at least one occasion, along with a physical training instructor from Barry, Glamorgan, I was involved in the collecting of data concerned with fallout which had been deposited on the ship. This involved the ship cruising downwind of the explosion and entering the fallout shadow.'

Keither Syder:

'On our return voyage a sprinkler system was working on deck. It was throwing water up and outwards. I believe this was to see how effectively the radioactivity was being dispersed. I know that on the first trip through the cloud I could see the dust settling on the anti-slip pads on deck. ... I would estimate that the total voyage through and back through the cloud took about four hours, although I can't be absolutely specific. I did not go below until the end of the return voyage, which was the end of the duty. After we had emerged from the cloud on our return voyage the sprinklers were turned off and the decks were hosed down. No attempt was made to clean the sumps, gun turrets, drainage sections or other cavities.'

Howard Coles:

'Protective clothing for my companion and myself was limited to anti-gas oilskins, an anti-flash balaclava, and a gas mask which had to be removed when data from the geiger counters was relayed to the central control. We were obliged to remain on deck during the period of monitoring, in which certain sections of the ship were deemed to be "hot", and so required extra attention during the period of the test.'

There was no lack of fallout for *Diana* to steam through. Mosaic 2 had been a big bomb (as atom bombs go) and it had made a big cloud: so big that it met different winds at different heights. The cloud split. The greater part got blown out to sea but the smaller part (or part of the smaller part) drifted across the mainland. Parts of the coast were contaminated, and for the next few days aircraft flew sampling missions throughout the area. Well, they might have flown those missions anyway just as a precaution; and the contamination seems to have been very light indeed and often scarcely measurable. But there's no denying the fact that *some* of the cloud had gone east when *all* of it was scheduled to go west, so to that extent the test went wrong. To put it another way: if everybody had known in advance that the cloud was going to split and part of it was going to cross the mainland, would Mosaic 2 have gone ahead? Obviously not. What happened was not what was intended to happen. It was a mistake.

DECAY AND DECEIT

In the end, the existence or non-existence of the *bloody hell* telegram isn't terribly important. What is revealing is the fact that the Australian Royal Commission saw fit to question Lord Penney and Vice Admiral Martell about it at all, and that neither of them reacted with amazement and incredulity at the notion of the Australian Prime Minister slagging off the British Prime Minister. Lord Penney's response was to say: *if it happened I think I would have remembered it.* He did not say: *I never heard of anything so bizarre and improbable! Don't you realise that our relations with our Australian allies were at all times so genial and cordial that the very idea of such a telegram is as unthinkable as the meeting of parallel lines?* He didn't say it, because it wasn't true. Relations between Britain and Australia during the 1950s were not always as good as they might have been. There were times when the Australian government suspected the British government of keeping an ace up its sleeve, and the Australians were right. The fact that it was sometimes the fifth ace in the pack didn't redeem matters, either.

A clue to this relationship is contained in a letter that Sir William Penney, as he then was, sent to Sir Frederick Brundrett at the Ministry of Defence on 22 December 1955.

'We think that it is likely that the Australians will ask us for filters which have been flown at Mosaic and Buffalo.

163

[Mosaic and Buffalo were 1956 operations, so the filters – cloud samples – had not yet been taken; Penney was looking ahead.] No doubt they will offer very close security treatment in their Atomic Energy Commission. While I am not very keen on the idea of giving them samples, I do not see how we can refuse. They could, of course, fly 'planes of their own or they could most easily take contaminated soil particles from the close in area.

'They would not know that fall out contamination from close in areas is very different from samples obtained from the cloud, and that only the latter is sufficiently representative to enable quantitative estimates to be made. On the other hand, they are probably very puzzled to know why we fly 'plane to get samples when it would be very much easier to take a few shovelfuls of dirt from the crater.

'On balance I am recommending that if they ask us we give them a little piece of the filters, but that we wait a few days so that some of the short-lived key isotopes have decayed a good deal.'

Clearly this was not an example of a full and free exchange of information between the two countries. Giving the Australians a little piece of much-decayed filter – and passing it off as the real thing – smacks of deceit, if not fraud.

When Mr McClelland, President of the Australian Royal Commission, read the letter at the London hearings and pointed out that Lord Penney had not been frank and open with the Australians, Lord Penney had to agree. But, he explained, this was weapons diagnostics, which was not the same thing as how big was the weapon, and that sort of thing. (By which he meant that the Australians didn't need the information for their safety procedures.)

The next question was obvious. Mr McClelland asked why he didn't take the frank and open course of telling the Australians that this information was weapon diagnostics and could not be made available? Lord Penney explained that at that stage the Australians hadn't asked him. He thought it likely that they would.

Mr McClelland: 'Why didn't you say, "Well, if they do ask us, I think it would be better that we tell them if we cannot give them this material, because it is weapons design", rather than take the course which you would agree, I think, involves a deception?'

Lord Penney: 'If I had said that, I think they would have been cross, and they could have said, "All right, we'll go and get some for ourselves". That would have put some friction into the machine . . .'

POWER POLITICS

Up to a point, Lord Penney. The machine which Britain was desperately anxious to lubricate was Anglo–American. During the war Britain and America had worked together on the Manhattan Project, but since then America had kept her nuclear secrets to herself and Britain had been left in the cold. One purpose of the 1950s tests was to show Washington (and Moscow, of course) that Britain was a full member of the nuclear club and therefore deserved to go back into partnership with America. And there was another purpose. The 1950s were a rackety decade (Korea, Suez, Hungary) and Britain's military leaders lived with the idea of nuclear war. They wanted the bomb and they had to have it fast. Everyone knew there was going to be a ban on atmospheric testing soon – too much fallout was circling the world already. The bomb Britain wanted was the real bomb, the hydrogen bomb. But it takes an atom bomb to detonate a hydrogen bomb. Therefore the scientists had to perfect this trigger device. That's what Operation Mosaic was all about. Penney's men had to test the triggers at Monte Bello in 1956 so as to be sure they would detonate the H-bomb at Christmas Island in 1957. And they had to do it fast. Mosaic 1 and 2 were organized with great urgency. Unfortunately no amount of human urgency could change the weather.

Britain exploded 21 nuclear weapons in Australia or the Pacific. Fifteen of those tests took place in the period August to November – six in September, seven in October. There was a good reason for this: the prevailing winds at that time of year were the most suitable. Operation Hurricane, the HMS *Plym* test, had been held in October 1952. Now the scientists proposed to hold Mosaic in May and June – the Australian winter, when the winds commonly blew from the west and forecasting was difficult even when they didn't.

Mosaic 1 went off without too much trouble on 16 May 1956. Then the weather became fickle. If it didn't settle down in June the outlook was very poor, because July is a dependably stormy month in that part of the world. Bernard Perkins, who served on the command ship HMS *Narvik*, described in his statement to the Commission the sense of tension on board:

> 'There were 3 or 4 abortive countdowns before the second explosion. Everybody was getting very fed-up, and one or two sailors were taken off the ship, to hospital, since they had breakdowns. Another person was taken off because he had started behaving as a homosexual. There was very great tension in the air. I remember talking to one scientist who was working on a timing device. He said that the long wait was because the weather had to be right. But they had to hurry because of time and money. He said that the weather was about to close up and the winds change. He said that if the second explosion was going to take place it would have to happen soon and that if it did not, it would be the most tremendous waste of time and money.'

Well, the scientists got their trigger (although there is reason to think that they were embarrassed by its size) and the inhabitants of Dampier, Roebourne and Broome in West Australia got a taste of radiation. But was Mosaic 2 an example of the way human fallibility can influence even something as hugely important as when – or whether – to set off an atomic bomb? Especially a very dirty bomb? One of the

166

things that strikes me about Mosaic 2 is that, for a trigger device, it made a vast amount of fallout. When triggers were used to detonate H-bombs at Christmas Island the explosions took place at height; but Mosaic 2 wasn't tested at height; it was tested on a 100-foot scaffolding tower. When he appeared before the Australian Royal Commission Lord Penney had this to say: 'The military, as I keep stressing, were thinking about nuclear war and in nuclear war the weapons would be to attack the enemy and do as much harm to him as possible; and a ground burst was a very likely way.' Mosaic 2 wasn't exactly a ground burst but it was the next worst thing. Could it be that the aim was to test two for the price of one: a trigger for the H-bombs *and* a dirty bomb for HMS *Diana*?

OUTLOOK GRIM

And when time began running out and the gales of July got closer, the awful prospect loomed of having to cancel Mosaic 2, dismantle the tower, recover all the scientific equipment, remove the weapon, dismiss the fleet, send *Diana* all the way back home, and perhaps have to face the Government with the news that the H-bomb programme would be delayed until the trigger device was a sure thing. The pressure to take a chance on the weather must have been strong. After all, no forecast is guaranteed, so there's always an element of risk. But in this case, the risk from the changeable weather was multiplied by the sheer size of the bomb – certainly four times, and perhaps more than six times, as powerful as Mosaic 1. The bigger the explosion, the bigger the error – if there is an error. On board *Narvik*, Bernard Perkins witnessed the effects of both factors: the wind, and the size of the burst:

'The cloud from the second explosion began moving away from the Australian mainland, but then changed direction and drifted back across the mainland. There was a big geiger counter on the aft deck which went berserk after the second explosion. There was also one in the

167

superstructure. My recollection is that it was ticking for a few days after the bomb, weaker all the time.'

Lord Penney stands by the decision to go ahead with Mosaic 2, just as he stands by the decision to fire a much earlier kiloton-range device. This was called Totem 1 and it was exploded at Emu Field in South Australia on 14 October 1953. At the London hearings Mr McClellan put it to Lord Penney that he had known there was considerable risk of contamination falling to the ground within 150 miles of Emu Field when the decision was taken to fire Totem 1. Lord Penney disagreed. Mr McClellan suggested that in the circumstances Totem 1 should not have been fired. Lord Penney disagreed. But when a man called Ronald Siddons came to be questioned, a different story emerged.

Siddons was a mathematician; his job at Emu Field was to help calculate what would happen when Totem 1 went off, and he co-authored a report predicting its results. He told the Commission: 'I believe that it was unduly risky to proceed with Totem One at the time it was fired. If I had been asked at the time, my advice would have been not to run the risk.' Ronald Siddons is now a Deputy Director of the AWRE at Aldermaston.

30 MINUTES FROM BEATING IT TO HAWAII

If an error of judgement of this sort could be made at Emu Field or Monte Bello, could it also be made at Christmas Island? Too many veterans speak of 'the bomb that went wrong' for it to be dismissed as an enjoyably morbid rumour, like the radioactive floods that were said to have followed one test and which certainly never happened. It's surprisingly difficult to pinpoint which bomb was 'the bomb that went wrong'; but cross-bearings from several accounts seem to indicate the H-bomb test known as Grapple 7, which took place on 28 April 1958 – not the ideal time of year, as Mosaic 2 had shown. Donald Ward, who witnessed that test, recalls: 'They were very concerned because the wind was changing and we were told it might blow the cloud over the island.'

Tony Crossland was much more closely involved with events:

'After one of the H-blasts the wind changed direction and the cloud came back at the island. Being in the RAF Police I was told that if the wind didn't change back to the original direction it would be necessary to evacuate the island, and we were within about half an hour of this when the wind went back.'

About the evacuation plan, Tony Crossland says:

'This appears in retrospect almost criminal. We were aware that if anything were to go radically wrong we would have to get off the island, but all we knew was that in such an event everyone would be taken to Port London where we would get on board anything that floated and set off north towards the Hawaiian islands, 1200 miles away.'

There is another candidate for 'the bomb that went wrong': the Guy Fawkes burst. Alex Hart was a 20 year old National Serviceman, a blacksmith in REME, when he witnessed the H-bomb test on 8 November 1957. His unit was grouped near the Main Camp on the north of the island, with a row of vehicles between them and the explosion as a blast barrier.

'When the bomb went off we were standing with our backs to it with our Jungle Greens on and our sun glasses and a sweat band round our necks.

'We turned and faced the bomb at the count of 10 and when the blast came, palm trees were sent flying through the air like matches. The next thing I knew we were thrown into the air like leaves.

'When our OIC Major Jones got us all together he said he had never seen anything like it during the last war. That

169

night no dinner was laid on as the Cook House had received damage. We had sandwiches instead.

'Sir William Penney gave a talk in the camp "cinema" that evening about leading the world with H-bombs and about the little mistake that was made earlier that day.'

ONLY 10% OUT ... OR 20%

I asked Alex Hart what exactly Sir William said was the cause of the 'little mistake'. He said that his talk was less about the mistake than about how well the tests were going and how far ahead of Russia Britain was in the nuclear race. This may have been meant as a pep-talk to counter the Russian achievement of launching the first man-made satellite, Sputnik. It was clearly visible from Christmas Island and attracted much attention as it passed overhead at night – especially from the audience in the open-air cinema during a bad film.

A special souvenir issue of *Mid Pacific News* celebrated the Guy Fawkes H-bomb as part of what it called 'the scientific onward march of man'. It said nothing about damage from blast, but it had a paragraph about the importance of photographing the explosion with cameras 'pre-set to look at exactly the right place in the sky. This implies that the Valiant must be able to put the bomb right on the bulls-eye without fail which it does with amazing accuracy.' That, like everything else in the souvenir issue, had been written before the event. Of course it's very possible that the drop was perfect but the bomb was not. Lord Penney has been quoted as saying that the error in megaton-range explosions – that is, H-bombs – was never more than 10 per cent or 20 per cent. Whether or not you find that reassuring depends on the size of the base figure. Ten per cent of a 1-megaton explosion is only the difference of a big atom bomb, whereas twenty per cent of a 10-megaton explosion is two million tons of TNT. As always, until the Ministry of Defence allows, or better yet instructs, the AWRE to give a full account of each explosion, any debate is stifled by ignor ance. That doesn't resolve the argument. You don't convince people by silencing them.

THE LAW (OR WHAT'S LEFT OF IT)

If the Christmas Island veterans are so convinced that they got hurt by radiation, why don't they take the Ministry of Defence to court and sue for damages on the grounds of negligence?

There are two answers to that. The first is the Crown Proceedings Act 1947. Strictly speaking, this doesn't prohibit a serviceman (which includes ex-servicemen) from suing the Crown for negligence on the grounds that the injury was caused by another serviceman, such as the Commander-in-Chief, while he (the first serviceman) was on duty. It just makes such a suit virtually impossible. According to the Act, once the Secretary of State for Social Services has issued a certificate saying that the serviceman's injury is 'attributable to injury for purpose of pension entitlement', the Crown is in the clear. It can't be sued. (What's more, issuing the certificate doesn't guarantee that any pension will be awarded. All it means is that the DHSS will look at the case.) So, at the first whiff of a civil suit by an ex-serviceman, the MOD can nudge the DHSS, a certificate will be in the post and the suit dies at birth.

It is not quite as appalling as it sounds. There were good reasons in 1947 for the Crown Proceedings Act. Firstly, service in the armed forces is patently risky, and servicemen know what they're getting into. What's more, if every soldier took the Crown to court whenever his jeep (driven by another man) rolled over, the legal system would be awash in actions for tort. Secondly, the armed forces have systems for compensating men who get hurt in the line of duty, and it would be intolerable if the taxpayer had to pay twice over for the same injury.

171

RECKLESS OR NEGLIGENT?

With Christmas Island, of course, there is a difference. National Servicemen knew about the risks of service but they hadn't volunteered for it; the State had conscripted them. Moreover the long-term effects of radiation are not like the conventional hazards of Service life. Christmas Island was a special case (so the argument goes) and deserves special treatment.

That cuts no ice with the lawyers, which is the second reason why nobody in Britain has even tried to sue the MOD – so far. The problem would be to prove negligence, and negligence is a word that is very closely defined in the civil courts. In a nutshell, it means that somebody failed to do something that he knew he should do (or did something that he knew he shouldn't do) and as a result someone else suffered. The defence of what happened at Christmas Island and elsewhere is simple: those in charge were acting *according to the best information available at the time*. What they did may turn out to be wrong, thirty years later; but that doesn't make them negligent. For instance, I might claim that it was reckless and irresponsible to sail HMS *Diana* through a fallout cloud, but those words wouldn't get me very far in a civil case for negligence against the captain, the Admiralty or the MOD – which means against the Crown.

There's been an interesting development in recent years in civil cases against places like Sellafield, *née* Windscale. The court has listened with sympathy to the argument that the *balance of probability* points to the injury or death having been caused by radiation in the place of work. Total cast-iron proof wasn't required (and in that sort of case, of course, total cast-iron proof is usually impossible). There may be a gleam of encouragement here for the Christmas Island veterans. But no more than a gleam. Before you start talking about balance of probability, you still have to prove negligence. And personally, I think it will be a cold day in hell before the MOD lets a negligence suit get to court.

172

OBJECT OF THE EXERCISE

'The Army must discover the detailed effects of various types of explosion on equipment, stores and men with and without various types of protection.'

Report on Atomic Weapon Trials by the Defence Research Policy Committee to the Chiefs of Staff Committee, 20 May 1953.

Mark Mildred asked Lord Penney how he interpreted the requirement described above.

Lord Penney: How I interpreted it was in my mind there was never any question of putting men, real men, into danger. That was in my mind. How do you measure the effect on men? First of all, you show them the thing from a safe distance. Do they panic? Do they look worried? What is their reaction to that? That is one thing. How do you find out what happens to a man at a close distance, where a real man would be burnt or injured? So what do you do then? You make models of men and you stick them in jeeps, lie them on the ground. We had a lot of that. That is another way. The next thing you do is you measure the heat because an airburst bomb close by is terrible for heat. So we have heat-sensitive paper . . .

Mark Mildred: That is not really what it says, is it? They want to discover the detailed effects of various type of explosions on men?

Lord Penney: Looking at this now, I would say that drafting was pretty dreadful because it can lead to mis-understandings. You have made the point on that and I accept that but to me that was not what was meant. There were two meanings to these words and when you are drafting something as important as this you do not want ambiguity and that has ambiguity, I accept, but it did not have any ambiguity to me.

* * *

173

The night before the second H-bomb was due to be dropped near Christmas Island (28 April 1958), two aircrew officers came to Ron Hunt, a pharmacist. They said they had the Medical Officer's permission to collect two Black Medical Eye Shades (commonly called eye patches) for each of them. The eye shades were in boxes of medical stores that had been packed up and stacked in a lorry in case of evacuation. While the officers shone torches, Ron Hunt searched the lorry and found the eye shades. The officers told him they needed them to protect their eyes from the flash of the bomb. 'This incident,' Ron Hunt suggests, 'puts the protective-clothing issue into perspective!'

Or semi-perspective. For, if each officer wore two black patches he would be unable to see anything – not a helpful condition for aircrew. You might as well wear a blindfold and be done with it. So what was going on? William McNamara, now living in County Down, put me straight. He wore a black patch when he was at – or rather above – Christmas Island.

Mr McNamara was on the island in April 1958. He was a navigator with 240 Squadron RAF, flying Shackletons. They flew weather patrols and shipping patrols around the test area. At the scheduled time of the blast, all the crew of the Shackleton bar two would be safely tucked away in parts of the plane which the flash could not reach. The two exceptions were the pilot and the navigator. The pilot was at the controls and the navigator was beside him.

At the instant of detonation, the Shackleton should be flying *away* from the explosion. However, there was a risk of premature detonation. Therefore the pilot and the navigator each wore one black eye-patch. If they were caught by the flash, the other eye would be blinded but they would each still have one good eye with which to fly the aircraft.

Ron Hunt issued four eye-patches – enough for two Shackletons. Presumably the rest of the squadron took their chances.

'Never did we get any instruction as regards ill effects, after effects (of radiation). We did however have a pep talk by our Staff Sergeant Major who said in no uncertain terms, "If any more men go sick with nothing to show, I will have them in the nick for wasting the MO's time!"'

> Peter Kennedy, Sapper on Christmas Island.
> Letter.

It would not be fair to say that the average serviceman on Christmas Island got a poor education in the effects of radiation. He got no education at all. It's true that a few were given a few lectures, but they were very few and some of what they were told was of dubious value. (For instance Brian Gillman and his fellow Sappers on Malden Island were told that their film badges would change colour in the presence of radioactivity, which was not the case.) When Dr Stevenson spoke of 'accepted risk' and said 'it depends how far you explain it, and obviously this depends on the intellect of the individual', he sounds as if he's living in another world. National Servicemen were not all fools. Some were graduates or were going onto university; some had completed apprenticeships. Precious little explaining went on, no matter what the intellect of the individual. Bernard Perkins remembers:

'I did not know exactly what was happening except that we were going to the atomic tests at Monte Bello island. We were told that we would be paid one shilling per day danger money, but we thought that was for the danger associated with the explosion rather than the radioactivity.'

Nobody came down with radiation sickness on Christmas Island, but if they had, it's highly unlikely that a military doctor would have recognised it – assuming, that is, that the man saw a doctor. Mr N. Wright, who was a Sapper with 59 Airfield Construction Company from November 1957 to November 1958, never saw a doctor in his whole tour of duty,

175

not even when he stood on a nail and his poisoned leg 'swelled up like a balloon'. Medical attention, he recalls, was 'very basic. Coral sores, which were quite prevalent, were treated with a scrubbing brush and soap, followed by a dressing of surgical spirit.'

Jack Kearney – the diver who swallowed some water in Monte Bello lagoon and was asked by the ship's doctor if he thought he had an atomic stomach – returned to Britain, still in pain.

'I was sent to see the doctor in RN Barracks, Guzz [Naval slang for Plymouth]. He said I had a large abnormal stomach. The following day I was picked up by ambulance and taken to RN Hospital Stonehouse, Plymouth. After tests the doctor told me I had a d. ulcer. After about 8 weeks of treatment another doctor sent for me and told me there was nothing wrong with me. After being told this I blew my top and told the doctor I was writing to my MP. In the afternoon a nurse told me not to write to my MP as on Admiral's Rounds on Wednesday the Admiral was personally reviewing my case. The following day after seeing the Admiral the medical board sent for me and I was discharged on medical grounds, and I received a 20% war pension.'

(Letter.)

Graham Mabbutt, the petty officer who got splashed on the arms and legs with liquids leaking from drums of radioactive waste matter, came back to the UK on HMS *Zeebrugge*.

'Shortly after the return voyage I began to suffer from a form of psoriasis on the forearms, and a nervous state, which is quite foreign to my nature. I got into the nervous state about six months after I returned to England. I was then a Boys Instructor, with absolutely no job stress at all. The doctor told me to leave the ship. I went to the Royal Naval Hospital at Haslar. I saw a skin consultant who appeared to think that my skin condition was of a nervous origin. At no time was I asked if I had served at Monte Bello and at risk from radiation. For that matter I did not think to mention it.'

If there was a Christmas Island disease it was persistent diarrhoea. 'Screamer's paradise' was the nickname LAC Terry Hooper remembered. Another airman, wireless fitter John Barnes, recalled two weeks when he was between jobs with nothing to do:

'. . . and spent the whole time looking for a vacant thunderbox as the whole island was down with the runs. Never did find an empty one so used one of the two spades every tent had been issued with for that purpose. When you got the cramps you dashed from the tent collecting the spade on the run, ran as far from the tent lines as circumstances would allow, squat, and swat (the flies), cover the mess and on the way back pass the spade to whoever was dashing towards you.'

*　　*　　*

During the London hearings, Mark Mildred was questioning Mr W. G. McDougall about protective standards and monitoring procedures at Maralinga, when they got onto an item in Mr McDougall's report:

'There were a number of cases of people entering the forward area and receiving appreciable doses when their tasks might well have been postponed or not have been done at all.'

That, he explained, related to a disagreement he had had with 'one or two senior military officers who previously [sic] thought, because their men were exposed to it, they should be exposed to it.' Mark Mildred went on to suggest that this was an example of what the Americans call the hairy-chested approach. Mr McDougall said he supposed so, yes.

From what I can see, there was a lot of the hairy-chested

approach to the finer points of radiation medicine at the British nuclear tests.

THE FALL AND FALL OF THE DOSE

Hitler wasn't the only man reducing the life expectancy of German youth in 1944. A German country doctor was doing his bit with a drug called Peteosthor, which he recommended strongly for patients who had TB. Many were children.

Peteosthor was a radioactive preparation containing radium 224, and about two thousand patients got repeated intravenous injections of it. It made absolutely no difference to their TB, but it produced a lot of malignant tumours of the bone, a certain amount of fatal kidney disease, probably some fatal liver disease, and several cataracts.

German hospitals went on administering Peteosthor to TB patients until 1951. It may seem medieval that doctors could pump radioactivity into their patients' veins without giving thought to the possibility of cancers being formed, but it happened and not so very long ago. Between the wars radium was a fashionable cure-all in the United States, rather like multivitamins today; people kept a bottle of radium pills on the bedside table and popped one whenever they felt a little low. So the idea that radioactivity is bad for you is recent.

Even after Hiroshima it took a long time for the message to get home. On 29 June 1950 a British scientist wrote a letter, no longer secret, that contains an aside which is more revealing than the rest of the contents. The letter is from Dr John Loutit of the Radiobiological Research Unit at the Atomic Energy Research Establishment, Harwell, to Sir Ernest Rock Carling at the Home Office.

Dr Loutit writes about the maximum dose of radiation the general public should receive (presumably in wartime). He goes on:

'If these doses should be exceeded in practice and it was felt that morale was suffering the defence would be: the figures contain safety factors and it is only the safety

178

factor that has been neutralised by exceeding the permissible dose. (This is not entirely true, but it is an argument that could be put across.)'

There is something breathtaking about the easy way the ethics of a public relations agency are applied to the effects of nuclear war, as if making people think they are safe is as good as making them safe.

Later in this letter Dr Loutit refers to Civil Defence emergency work when risks will have to be taken. 'My personal opinion is that the officer commanding will require to know chiefly – *that dose of radiation which will not cause invalidity.* Current medical opinion is that this dose is 25r.' He explains that the evidence for this figure comes from experiments on rabbits and on human volunteers. (It would be interesting to know who the volunteers were and whether any of them survive. It would also be interesting to know exactly what Dr Loutit meant by *invalidity*.)

A dose of 25r (assuming 'r' to mean roentgen) in 1950 was the most radiation a male worker should get in a year, according to the ICRP (International Commission on Radiological Protection) except that the ICRP didn't work it out by the year, they worked it out by the week and in 1950 they said that a male worker shouldn't get more than 0·5 roentgen per week. Since the MOD got its standards of protection for the nuclear tests from the ICRP, it's worth looking at the way ICRP dose limits have fallen in fifty years.

Different standards apply to different bits of the body – the eye is reckoned to be tougher than the gonads – so for the sake of simplicity I've chosen the ICRP dose limits for the whole body per week. Roentgen and rem are virtually equal.

1934	1 roentgen
1950	0.5 roentgen
1954	0.3 rem
1965	0.23 rem (3 rem/quarter)
1977	0.096 rem (5 rem/year)

It's all more complicated than that – everything to do with radiation is complicated – but it serves to show how dose limits have plunged in fifty years. What was considered a week's dose of radiation in 1934 would be a ten-week dose today.

NOTHING IS SAFE EXCEPT NOTHING

But if what has happened to *maximum* doses is startling, that's nothing compared to the disappearance of *minimum* doses. As late as the Fifties, many radiation biologists firmly believed that there was such a thing as a minimum dose – a safe level of radiation, below which no harm could come to anybody. This was the famous threshold, and for a time it eased the burden of health physics experts enormously. It meant that men could be slightly irradiated, and as long as the dose was below the threshold there was no need to do anything about it.

However, there was one inconvenient fact. In 1947 D. G. Catcheside had reported to the Medical Research Council that 'even the smallest doses of radiation produce a genetic effect, there being no threshold dose below which no genetic effect is induced.' That, of course, left the scientists with half a threshold, which was a nonsense, since soldiers cannot be semi-immune any more than women can be semi-pregnant.

Nevertheless, the threshold philosophy hung about like mist and there is no knowing how much influence it had on the way servicemen were monitored on Christmas Island – or, more likely, *not* monitored, since there's no point in checking the exposure of a bloke who's under the limit anyway.

I say there's no knowing. What I mean is there's no knowing outside the archives of the Ministry of Defence. Government spokesmen have repeatedly claimed that ICRP standards applied. All such information should be made public in full. Assurances are not enough. That applies to Christmas Island just as it has applied to Windscale/Sellafield.

DUNSTER SPEAKS! TWICE!

On 11 September 1958 Britain was exploding the last and biggest H-bomb in the whole series. By coincidence, on the other side of the world, on that very day, scientists from many countries had gathered to discuss the large-scale use of atomic energy and how it affected the environment. Representing Britain was a man called John Dunster, from the UK Atomic Energy Authority. There had recently been an 'incident' (a fire, in fact) at Windscale, and Mr Dunster was asked whether low-level wastage was purified before release, and whether it wouldn't be wise to limit release until more is known about what happens to radioactive waste in the sea. He replied:

'. . . In fact the discharges at Windscale have been treated from time to time – they are not treated continuously; it depends on the amount of radioactivity arising for disposal – but in general terms the intention has been to discharge fairly substantial amounts of radioactivity as part of an organised and deliberate scientific experiment and the aims of this experiment would in fact have been defeated if the level of activity discharged had been kept to a minimum.

'This leads to the second question, that it is actually unwise to discharge radioactivity into the sea indiscriminately, and only careful scientific evaluation of these problems can demonstrate the safety. One of the principal and, I believe, the most effective methods of carrying out these investigations is indeed to use radioactivity and discharge it and find out what happens to it.'

Well, that was in 1958. Would the standards of the 1950s be acceptable today? Would we still be happy to see 'substantial amounts of radioactivity' deliberately pumped into the Irish Sea on the breezy principle of use it and lose it and see what happens to it? As I write, British Nuclear Fuels Limited are being fined £10,000 for discharging material into the Irish Sea when its level of radioactivity was 'not as low as reasonably achievable'. Plus £60,000 costs. (It might have been more but the judge said he realised that BNFL's funds come from the public via taxes. When BNFL blunders, the public pays twice.)

181

I raise all these questions because John Dunster is now Director of the NRPB (who, you remember are making that study of nuclear veterans' health for the MOD) and in 1985 he told the Australian Royal Commission that:

'. . . *any* radiation exposure is presumed to cause *some* additional risk and all modern radiation protection policy is based on that presumption.'

When, I wonder, did 'modern' times begin? Were the 1950s – the decade of the British tests – modern? Or did the concept of a radiation threshold still hold sway then?

*　　*　　*

DIRTY WORK ON THE HIGH SEAS

Harold Brown should be dead. I know I can say that without offending him because he was the one who told me he should be dead. He got this information direct from his doctors who said in 1983 that he had two years left. That time limit expired in April 1985 but Mr Brown did not. When I went to see him at his home in Yeovil he seemed fiercely determined to go on living for a long time yet, and perhaps that's what is keeping him alive: sheer determination, laced with no small amount of anger and indignation that his country could treat him as he says it has and then deny everything.

He joined the Navy in 1943 when he was 17. Ten years later he was helmsman on board HMS *Starling*, not so much a warship as a training vessel. She took officers or cadets on navigational training courses. Most voyages were short: a couple of days at sea, then back to port. No sweat for the crew. A cushy posting.

In August 1953 she sailed from Portsmouth to Oban to Londonderry and then out into the Atlantic. Purpose of voyage: training course officers by carrying out dummy anchorages. That never happened, according to Harold Brown.

'I thought it was very funny when they got rid of the course officers on board the ship and they took RAF personnel on board. They don't do dummy anchorages from aircraft, do they?

'After we proceeded out into the Atlantic, we were told that we were going to have a wash-down programme with atomic dust. We were told to get below decks, and I did hear an aircraft in the vicinity of the ship. You know, to hear an aircraft, with the engines of the ship going, you know, the aircraft would have to be low, believe you me.

'When we came up on the upper deck there was dust on the upper deck. It was a reddy-brown and it had little specks of grey in it. And we were told it was atomic dust and we had to wash it down.

'We rigged the fire-hoses on board the ship and we set to, to wash it down, but we had great difficulty because of the breakwater on the bows and also the scuppers were not recessed into the deck, they were protruding above the deck. We were told that the wash-down procedure was to find out how they could redesign ships and things like that for . . . in case of atomic warfare, which the Navy were pushing at that time.'

Robinson: Who told you all this?

'The bosun on board the ship said that the dust we were washing down was atomic dust, and he also said that we had to mix some of the dust with pussers grey paint and paint the seaboats, plus the fact that we had to put a plank over the side and paint part of the side of the ship, which was a strip about six foot wide – you know, it was the length of the plank that we had, to go down and paint.'

Robinson: Did you make this mixture?

'I made the mixture, I picked the dust up and mixed it up into the pots of paint that we used.'

Robinson: How much dust?

'As far as I can recall, I put about two handsful of dust per pot of paint, and mixed it up to paint the side of the ship.'

Robinson: How many pots of paint?

'We're talking about six pots of paint altogether. You know, painting the seaboats, painting the side of the ship. Yes.'

Robinson: Did that get rid of all the dust?

'Well, no, no, no. It was an impossible situation, trying to wash the dust down off the upper deck anyway. A funny thing happened when we did eventually get back into Portsmouth again. They put tarpaulins around the ship. . . . First of all, they got rid of the seaboats. Seaboats vanished from the ship. Then, when we got into dry dock, they put canvas sheets completely round the whole of the ship and – something that I've never, ever, in my life, seen before – a ship being high-pressure hosed down, in a dry dock. The entire ship, from the top of the mast downwards. It was completely washed down with high-pressure hoses. Also the side of the ship was chipped down and all the (new) paint was removed.'

After that, HMS *Starling* went back to her training role.

A GENEROUS HELPING OF FUDGE

On 11 February 1985 in the House of Commons, Paddy Ashdown – Harold Brown's MP – asked the Defence Secretary whether the log book of HMS *Starling* for the relevant period in 1953 had been withdrawn from the Public Records Office, and would he make a statement? Adam Butler replied. The ship's log for August, he said, had been withdrawn so that the MOD could answer Paddy Ashdown's letters about 'alleged radiation trials'. 'From this examination of this document it would appear that there are no grounds whatsoever for believing that such trials took place . . .'

Now that was a curious reply. It didn't actually say that no radiation trials took place on *Starling*; it said that according to the ship's log, *it would appear* that such trials did not happen. Presumably the MOD keeps records of its radiation trials. You would think that some junior under-secretary could check these records and report his findings, one way or the other: either *Starling* was involved in radiation trials or she wasn't. Clearly that's what Paddy Ashdown wanted to know. Equally clearly that's what the MOD didn't want to say.

Two days after the Parliamentary reply, Lord Trefgarne wrote to Paddy Ashdown about the *Starling* affair. (Lord Trefgarne was an Under-Secretary of State at the MOD.) He mentioned Adam Butler's reply and then went into some detail about what the ship's log recorded for August 1953: at Portsmouth until the 10th, then to Scottish waters to practise 'dummy anchorages'. Called at Oban, Tobermory, Londonderry, Falmouth, back to Portsmouth on the 28th. 'At no time did she proceed into the open Atlantic during that month and there is no record of her having taken scientists on board.'

Yes, yes, Lord Trefgarne, but what about radiation trials? Once again the official reply is deafening in its silence.

And there is the curious use of the word 'open' before 'Atlantic'. After Tobermory on the 16th, *Starling*'s next port of call was Londonderry on the 22nd. Sail from Tobermory to Londonderry and you sail through a corner of the Atlantic. What's more, *Starling* was in those waters for at least five days when a direct journey from Tobermory to Londonderry would have taken at the very most 24 hours. Finally, 'there is no record of her having taken scientists on board'. Everything is answered obliquely, with reference to the log, nothing is answered directly. That's the best way to handle it, don't you think? Yes, Minister.

ALL VERY UNUSUAL

Of course it is always possible that Harold Brown imagined everything. If so, he was not alone. I contacted two of his

185

shipmates who confirmed important details of his story. Ray Hobson clearly remembered civilians – the 'brolly and bowler brigade', he called them – coming aboard HMS *Starling*, with an escort of high-ranking RAF officers. Ray Hobson was a National Serviceman. He was one of the 'side party' in the crew whose job it was to keep their side of the ship spic-and-span; so the sight of what looked like red sand spread everywhere made a particular impression on him. Mr H. J. Metcalf was a stoker and so was below during the wash-down operation, but he recalled the ship's motorboat being painted; he was concerned with this because he was responsible for the motorboat's engine. He confirmed that the ship's boats and motorboat were removed before *Starling* entered drydock. This, he said, was very unusual. Indeed for *Starling* to go into drydock at all was most unusual. 'We were under sailing orders,' he said. 'If they know the ship's due to go into drydock it wouldn't be under sailing orders.'

If these three men independently invented the same story, they also invented what was in fact a standard (but secret) Admiralty practice for treating contaminated ships: sealing the radioactivity in with paint. Ian McKenzie was the ship's painter on board HMS *Tracker* in 1952. He remembers being in charge of the complete repainting of the ship when she returned to Devonport. He suspected at the time that this was 'to cover up and contain the radioactivity . . .' and he was right. Seven weeks after the Monte Bello explosion, a confidential letter from the flag officer commanding the special squadron informed the Admiralty that his ships had been decontaminated and 'any residual contamination is being sealed in by painting or varnishing . . .' But: 'In the case of HMS *Tracker* a further survey of the special compartments, followed if necessary by decontamination and painting, will be required on arrival in the United Kingdom . . .'

WHAT DO YOU BELIEVE?

There is one further possible explanation of the *Starling* stories. Perhaps there *was* a wash-down operation to get rid of a coating of 'atomic dust' – but perhaps this dust was harmless; perhaps it was dropped on deck not by an aeroplane but by the scientists, while most of the crew were below. It was all just an exercise, to test the cleansing system.

For a brief moment that has a kind of dotty plausibility. But the questions come rushing in. Where was all this fake dust stored? How was it distributed? Who did the work? (Not scientists, you can bet.) Why didn't this extraordinary business – one lot of men covering the upper deck with dust for another lot to wash off – become the talk of the ship? And if the stuff was harmless, why seal it in with paint? Why scrub down the ship with high-pressure hoses?

Harold Brown's version is more credible, especially when you link it with the experience of HMS *Diana* less than a year before. The fact that his account is not supported by *Starling*'s log proves nothing. As Paddy Ashdown has said: 'You would not expect to find the details of a top-secret mission in the log.'

In 1953 Harold Brown trusted his officers. 'I had complete confidence that the dust that we washed down, the dust that we used in the paint, was harmless. But today I'm suffering.' He is indeed. He was 28 when he was on the *Starling* in 1953, 31 when he left the Navy in 1956. For years after that he had a rash so severe that his skin bled when he rubbed it. Now he has a wasting bone disease which obliges him to wear a steel corset. In 1970 cataracts were diagnosed in both eyes. The circulation of his blood deteriorated until one leg had to be amputated. Several lengths of arteries have been replaced with plastic tubing. He has had two major heart attacks and three small strokes.

You would expect a man like that to be bedridden, helpless; but when I met Harold Brown he was very much on his feet. His mind was clear and his speech was crisp. He knew what he thought: that the radiation trial on HMS *Starling* ruined his health. For the Ministry of Defence he had nothing but contempt. 'They're as good as telling me I don't know what I'm talking about,' he said. 'I feel very bitter. You know, if they asked me to do something for my country now I wouldn't tie two pieces of string together for them. And that's how I feel. Very bitter.'

PRECEDENT

The more I thought about the HMS *Starling* affair, the less sense it made.

If no radiation trial was ever held, why doesn't the MOD just say so, in so many words, instead of brandishing the ship's log? On the other hand, if they did use the *Starling* for a radiation trial (and Harold Brown has no doubt that Sir William Penney was one of the party on board) then why choose a training sloop instead of a warship? It all seems thoroughly cockeyed.

Then I opened the *Observer* (2nd July 1985) and read that a year before, in the summer of 1952, the Navy had been carrying out some biological-warfare experiments off the Hebrides when they accidentally sprayed a 400-ton Fleetwood trawler with plague bacilli. And in 1979 Mr Francis Pym assured an MP it never happened. One should never underestimate the ingenuity of the MOD.

FILLETED FILES

Records don't tell everything. Sometimes they don't tell anything. When Brian Gillman, one of the Malden Island Sappers, gave evidence at the inquest in Cornwall into the death of another nuclear veteran, he said his Army paybook – the usual record of service life – had been gutted, emptied. 'There's a first page and a last page and nothing in between,' he said. Chris Noone served on Christmas Island. His medical documents are incomplete, with a section missing for 1957 when he was treated for blisters on his back; and the 'service abroad' section fails to include his third trip to the island. Mr D. P. H. Harman knows he was on Christmas Island from July 1957 to July 1958, but 'I can only give approximate dates as there is no official record in my Airman's Service Book, which I still have.' Henry Carter, who served at the 1952 Monte Bello test, cannot gain access to his medical file as 'it has been stripped': three-quarters of it has disappeared. Doctors treating him told him the file was 'private and classified'.

It would be tedious to go on with the list. The point has been made: how can anyone be sure that nothing went wrong when so many documents are incomplete?

SO WHAT?

When I set out to write this book I knew nothing about Christmas Island except that it was in the Pacific and we used to let off H-bombs there. I'd never even heard of Maralinga and Monte Bello. Thus I had the benefit of an open mind. Open because empty.

I know more now, partly through talking to scientists and doctors and reading their stuff, partly through meeting nuclear veterans and getting their stories down on miles of tape. During all this, several things have never ceased to amaze me.

One is the false impression that people in Britain had of the major operation, the Christmas Island tests. That name, and the fact that it is near the equator, told them it must be a tropical paradise. The veterans I met remembered only one visit by newsmen, and that was to see the Guy Fawkes explosion; after which they did not hang around. For two years, Christmas Island was one of the biggest British bases in the world, certainly the biggest Combined Operation, built and equipped at enormous speed and cost. Yet apart from an occasional celebratory column – 'Britain drops a REAL H-bomb' was one headline – Christmas Island was ignored. No doubt the MOD did not encourage visitors. Even so, its isolation was stark.

Another constant source of surprise is the radical change since then in attitudes towards authority. Today, the Fifties seem like an age of total public trust in a wise, paternal government. The word 'innocence' crops up. Tony Crossland looks back at 'those days when a combination of the innocence of youth and the power of Queen's Regulations resulted in one not querying an official order'. Brian Tate puts it more bluntly: 'Then you was in the Army, or the Forces, and they told you to

190

jump, you fucking jumped, didn't you? It's as simple as that. I mean it's different now, like now we talk about it, but . . . See, we couldn't turn round and say to 'em "No I ain't gonna do that" . . . Because, you know, you think, "Well, they know what they're doing . . ."' Or as Robert Malcomson puts it: 'Then we were innocents, now we're not quite.'

Christmas Island couldn't happen again, and not only because of the Test Ban Treaty. Men wouldn't tolerate those conditions – bedbugs, diarrhoea, boredom; weeks or months of work from dawn till dusk or, if you preferred, dusk till dawn. True, there were compensations – sun and swimming, no bull, plenty of fish – and some men quite enjoyed their stint. But thirty years later the world is much smaller. The news would get out, even if the newsmen couldn't get in. The British people would hear about The Massacre of the Birds, and that alone would be enough to cause a monumental stink.

The temperature of an atom bomb immediately after it has been detonated is at least one million degrees Centigrade. Within a few millionths of a second, the fireball appears. After one thousandth of a second it is a hundred feet across and has a temperature of three hundred thousand degrees Centigrade. To anyone five or six miles away, it would be about one hundred times more brilliant than the sun. That's just an atom bomb. Hydrogen bombs, of course, are much brighter.

Christmas Island has always been famous for its huge seabird colonies. When Captain Cook discovered the island he noted 'infinite numbers of a new species of tern' as well as boobies, men-of-war birds, tropic birds, curlews and sandpipers. When the British nuclear tests began, eighteen species of sea-bird regularly nested there, some in colonies numbering millions. They wheeled overhead in vast clouds: shearwaters and petrels, boobies and frigatebirds, heron, mallard, pintail duck, golden plover, curlew, tern, noddy and even an indigenous land bird, the Christmas Island warbler.

Servicemen turned their backs on the bomb and put their hands over their eyes. The birds, if they chanced to be looking towards the explosion, took the flash on the retina and were blinded. Barry Cotton recalled:

'. . . after the light flash – not a sound, nothing, then suddenly the air was filled with screaming birds who'd been blinded by the flash. They were crashing into the deck and the trees.'

Even the birds that were not looking directly at the explosion were likely to be blinded. Most birds' eyes are placed at the sides of their heads, giving them good all-round vision; thus at least one eye would catch the flash. Peter Kennedy wrote to me of: '. . . the thousands of birds I have bashed with a pick handle and then burnt, all blinded by the bomb.'

Often, this work was done by volunteers. Barry Cotton was one:

'. . . those of us naval personnel in the main camp party commandeered our lorry and driver and some heavy sticks and spades and went off into the interior of the island and did a bad day's work. We killed all the blind and maimed birds we could find and buried them. There were hundreds and they were beautiful but dead. I think we got drunk afterwards.'

Hundreds of thousands of blinded seabirds must have fallen into the sea. As many more must have been killed by heat and blast. The surviving birds were not in a position to learn from the experience, so the massacre was repeated for each of the nine bombs, which means that the nuclear tests killed millions of birds and blinded or otherwise damaged millions more, who could not fly and died of starvation. The folks back home didn't hear about that.

I suppose what puzzles me most about the whole test series is the fact that only the bombs were tested, not the men. Given that the Chiefs of Staff had been urged in 1953 to find out what different types of explosions did to equipment and men 'with and without various types of protection' (which Lord Penney says is ambiguous but which looks pretty straightforward to me) I would have expected them to see what effect nuclear explosions had on the men who witnessed them, both physiologically and psychologically. Yet there were no follow-up medical checks of any kind. After the test series the Services made no attempt to find out what being in the neighbourhood of several nuclear explosions did to their men. Even the crew of HMS *Diana*, which was repeatedly sailed through a fallout cloud, have not been given any follow-up tests.

On a practical level this seems an appalling waste of a unique opportunity. God knows it cost a fortune to hold the tests (Mosaic 2, alone, is said to have cost £1.5 million); why not get the most for your money by testing everything – men as well as weapons? They did it in the United States. Why not here? Recently (Hansard, 8 February 1983) the Prime Minister gave this answer:

> 'No special measures to monitor the long-term health of military personnel were taken because the radiation exposure records indicated that they had not been exposed to any significant health hazard.'

That is the most circular statement since the invention of the wheel. It rolls like this: *We haven't needed to check them because there's nothing wrong with them, and we know there's nothing wrong with them because that's why we don't need to check them.* It makes for an easier life: after all, when you know everything there's no point in trying to find out what you don't know.

*   *   *

Television news editors have a word for exciting bits of film: 'sexy'. It has nothing to do with sex but everything to do with action, violence, conflict, drama. (For instance, tank battles in the Middle East produce sexy footage.) Television news editors live in perpetual fear that, without sexy film at frequent intervals, viewers will quit. Television doesn't like what it calls 'talking heads'. Given a choice of stories, a news editor goes for the one with sexy film every time.

193

There is nothing sexy about the Christmas Island story. When you've seen one H-bomb, you've seen them all. After that there's nothing to do but look at the consequences; and, let's face it, middleaged men with cancer or cataracts, or young people with deformed bodies, are guaranteed to put the average viewer right off. He/she really doesn't want to know. Where's the action? Where's the drama? Who's the villain? What's the quick solution? There's no answer to those questions.

Without television, any ginger group has a tough row to hoe these days. BBC's 'Nationwide' and 'Panorama' and Channel 4's 'Broadside Company' did a fine job for nuclear veterans – but that was in 1982 and 1983. The trouble is, of course, that the villain in the story makes not only bad television but bad news in any medium, being silent, invisible, odourless, tasteless and in all respects except one non-existent. That one respect may prove to be lethal, but without the shock of a bloody knife or a smoking revolver it is difficult for the onlooker to feel threatened, alarmed or indignant. At an emotional level, most of us don't believe in radiation. We accept with our minds that it exists, just as we accept that the far side of the moon exists, but radiation is – in every sense of the word – unreal to us.

What's more, there's a kind of Catch-22 in the Christmas Island story. What prompted the veterans' campaign is also what hampers it. You feel ill? You believe your illness was radiation-induced? You want to kick up a fuss? You can't. You feel too ill. It's a grim paradox that I met up and down the country. It goes a long way towards explaining why the veterans' campaign has not been more successful.

At the same time, there are organisational failings that cannot be blamed on sickness – obvious weaknesses that would hold back any cause. You can't run an association without an accurate, up-to-date membership list. There's no point in having records unless those records are complete and accurate and quickly accessible. Above all, you get nowhere until you know what your aims are, and that means *specific*

194

aims. The BNTVA talks too much of 'recognition' without always saying exactly what should be recognized, and why, and how. Merely damning the government as a pack of rascals gets you nowhere. (By contrast the Australian nuclear veterans made a convincing case which won them support from a wide range of organisations and helped bring about a Royal Commission.) Indeed, I often felt there was in general too much talk and too little action within the BNTVA, as if indignation alone were held to be enough. (Sometimes I suspected that an ego was being taken on a trip.) It is a hard and awkward fact that the Association has no paid staff, and so the load of leadership falls on a few. Nevertheless, if it doesn't achieve something it will fade away. Nothing stands still. Some members of the Association think they *deserve* to win because they are in the right. Unfortunately life does not work like that.

But, whether they intended it or not, the nuclear veterans have done us all a great service by reminding us that when we began splitting the atom we were fooling about with the unknown. We still know a damn sight less about radiation than we *don't* know. There is a huge temptation to see in the nuclear flash, the fireball, the giant mushroom, a sign that man has joined the gods and now disposes of power beyond measure. The truth about the Christmas Island story is that it was as much farce as high drama. That is clear from the first part of this book. The tragedy of the story lies in the second part, the account of the radiation-shotgun effect – echoes of the bombs still rumbling painfully a generation later. Especially when part three shows that Monte Bello, Maralinga and Christmas Island were not always such smooth military operations. There were cock-ups and miscalculations. Things could go wrong; things did go wrong. And now it looks very much as if too many veterans are paying for it with their health and their lives, and maybe even the health and lives of their children, too.

APPENDIX I

ROLL OF HONOUR

British Nuclear Tests Veterans Association
Medical Study, 1985: notifications of member's death

Name	Cause of Death	Age	Test Site
John Allen	Leukemia	40	Christmas Island
Redvers Angwin	Leukemia	50	Monte Bello
Sidney Arkell	Cancer	46	Christmas Island
Albert Armstrong	Heart Disease	52	NK
Douglas Ashelford	Cancer	56	Maralinga
John Barnes	Heart failure	42	Monte Bello
M. B. Basey	Cancer	59	Christmas Island
Harold Benge	Cancer	65	Christmas Island
Norman Blackburn	Cancer	55	Christmas Island
Geoffrey Blower	Cancer	59	Christmas Island
S. P. Bolton	Cancer	47	NK
Peter Boothby	NK	58	NK
Frederick Broughton	Leukemia	61	Monte Bello
Harry Brown	NK	48	Christmas Island
L. G. Brown	Cancer	51	Hiroshima
R. Bryant	Cancer	46	NK
John Burke	Cancer	40	Christmas Island
Peter Catterson	Heart failure	50	Christmas Island
Henry Carlton	Cancer	50	Monte Bello

NK = not known

Name	Cause of Death	Age	Test Site
Kenneth Charney	NK	62	Christmas Island
D. Chubb	Cancer	55	Christmas Island
F. Clayton	Cancer	NK	NK
William Compton	Cancer	57	NK
D. Connell	Cancer	28	Christmas Island
Ronald Cross	Heart failure	48	Christmas Island
Robert Crow	Cancer	65	Christmas Island
Stuart Cull	Cancer	41	Christmas Island
Ernest Davis	Cancer	59	NK
Vivian Day	Cancer	56	Christmas Island
B. J. Delacoe	NK	50	Christmas Island
Eric Done	Cancer	54	Christmas Island
Harold Dovey	Cancer	63	Maralinga
Samuel Downing	Cancer	47	NK
Frederick Dyke	Cancer	61	Christmas Island
P. M. Eldridge	Cancer	47	Christmas Island
Anthony Elliott	Cancer	31	Christmas Island
R. Eslor	Cancer	44	Woomera
Alastair Findlay	Cancer	43	Christmas Island
Peter Finucane	Leukemia	25	Maralinga
John Fisher	Cancer	59	Christmas Island
Derrick French	Leukemia	63	Maralinga
Alfred Gardner	Cancer	54	Christmas Island
S. Garrett	Cancer	59	Christmas Island
Bernard Geoghan	Heart failure	49	Christmas Island
Hugh Gettings	NK	49	Monte Bello
William Goldsmith	Cancer	26	NK
G. J. P. Graham	Cancer	72	Christmas Island
Jack Graham	Stroke	51	NK

Name	Cause of Death	Age	Test Site
Joseph Greavey	Cancer	63	Christmas Island
J. Green	Cancer	39	Christmas Island
William Grigsby	Cancer	53	Maralinga
?. Hanton	Cancer	59	NK
W. E. Harding	Cancer	62	Christmas Island
Raymond Harness	Cancer	37	Christmas Island
John Harrison-Broadley	Cancer	53	Maralinga; Monte Bello
Edgar Haynes	Cancer	50	Christmas Island
T. F. Healy	Cancer	57	Christmas Island
Alan Hillman	Leukemia	59	NK
George Hinkley	Cancer	42	Christmas Island
T. L. Hinson	Cancer	47	Christmas Island
K. H. Houghton	Cancer	64	Christmas Island
George Hughes	Leukemia	50	NK
Cyril Ireland	Renal failure	59	Monte Bello
Peter Keegan	Cancer	33	Christmas Island
W. Kenyon	NK	62	Christmas Island
Alan Knapper	Cancer	38	Christmas Island
L. G. Knight	Cancer	NK	Maralinga
Ronald Lacey	Cancer	62	NK
William Ladd	Cancer	62	NK
E. Lamerton	Respiratory failure	66	NK
John Langlois	NK	64	Christmas Island
T. A. Lawrence	Cancer	39	Christmas Island
Philip Lloyd	NK	53	NK
Francis McCann	Heart failure	35	Christmas Island

Name	Cause of Death	Age	Test Site
K. H. McCormack	Heart failure	54	Monte Bello
Henry McLaughlin	Cancer	66	Christmas Island
Murdo Macleod	Cancer	78	Maralinga
George M'Ghie	Cancer	45	Christmas Island
Cecil Mabbett	Heart failure	47	Monte Bello
Andrew Mack	Cancer	28	Christmas Island
Kenneth Maddison	Cancer	39	Christmas Island
U. E. Matthews	Cancer	57	Monte Bello
W. Mears	Cancer	60	NK
Kenneth Measures	Cancer	54	Christmas Island
Bertram Miles	Cancer	62	Christmas Island
James Milne	Cancer	60	Monte Bello
R. A. Moulton	Cancer	43	Christmas Island
?. Myall	Cancer	NK	NK
John Newman	Heart failure	45	Christmas Island
James Newton	Cancer	36	Christmas Island
J. B. Nicell	Cancer	63	Christmas Island
G. S. Norman	Cancer	51	Monte Bello
P. Overton	Cancer	70	Christmas Island
G. P. Page	Cancer	57	Christmas Island
Robert Parry	Cancer	NK	NK
Hugh Paterson	Cancer	46	Christmas Island
Alan Penny	Cancer	46	Christmas Island
P. N. Phillips	NK	25	Maralinga, Monte Bello
Charles Plank	Cancer	50	Christmas Island
Raymond Platt	Heart failure	44	NK
Raymond Pollard	Cancer	67	Monte Bello
Stuart Pountney	Cancer	NK	NK

Name	Cause of Death	Age	Test Site
Robert Pressdee	NK	48	Christmas Island
Albert Preval	NK	60	Christmas Island
Raymond Pynegar	Cancer	55	NK
William Rettie	Cancer	48	Christmas Island
Norman Robertson	Cancer	52	Monte Bello
Robert Rolfe	Cancer	52	Bikini Atoll
Victor Rudland	Stroke	58	Monte Bello
R. D. Secretan	Cancer	60	Maralinga
Harold Shaw	Cancer	69	Maralinga
Philip Squire	Cancer	44	Christmas Island
Roy Stewart	Cancer	60	Christmas Island
George Taylor	Cancer	39	Monte Bello
Leonard Terry	Cancer	55	Maralinga
John Thomson	Cirrhosis	42	Christmas Island
Peter Thorogood	Cancer	47	Christmas Island
Harry Tindall	Cancer	44	Maralinga
V. G. Townsend	Cancer	52	Christmas Island
Frank Tucker	Cancer	53	Christmas Island
D. A. Turner	Cancer	61	Maralinga
W. F. Turner	Cancer	49	Christmas Island
Leonard Warner	Leukemia	53	Marshall Islands
David Watkins	Heart disease	43	Maralinga
G. A. Welch	Cancer	69	Christmas Island
W. White	Cancer	56	NK
Ernest Whitelock	Stroke	58	Monte Bello
Peter Whittle	Cancer	56	Hiroshima
John Wilkinson	Cancer	39	Christmas Island
F. Wilshire	Cancer	42	NK
Edward Wilson	Cancer	36	Christmas Island
Peter Wilson	Heart Failure	48	Maralinga

Name	Cause of Death	Age	Test Site
Joseph Woof	Cancer	46	Christmas Island
David Woolgar	Cancer	47	Maralinga
R. F. Woolven	Cancer	39	Christmas Island
John Wyvill	Leukemia	49	Christmas Island
R. F. Yeo	Heart failure	41	Christmas Island

APPENDIX II

Atmospheric Nuclear Tests in Australia and at Christmas Island 1952–1958

Code	Location	Date	Yield Range	Explosion Conditions
Hurricane	Monte Bello (off Trimouille Island)	3 Oct 1952	25 kt	Ocean surface burst (HMS *Plym*)
Totem 1	Emu	15 Oct 1953	10 kt	Tower mounted
Totem 2	Emu	27 Oct 1953	8 kt	Tower mounted
Mosaic G1	Monte Bello (Trimouille Island)	16 May 1956	15 kt	Tower mounted
Mosaic G2	Monte Bello (Alpha Island)	19 Jun 1956	60 kt	Tower mounted
Buffalo	Maralinga (One Tree)	27 Sep 1956	15 kt	Tower mounted
Buffalo	Maralinga (Marcoo)	2 Oct 1956	1.5 kt	Ground burst
Buffalo	Maralinga (Kite)	11 Oct 1956	3 kt	Air dropped – high air burst over land
Buffalo	Maralinga (Breakaway)	22 Oct 1956	10 kt	Tower mounted
Grapple 1	Malden Island Pacific	15 May 1957	Megaton	Air dropped – high air burst over ocean
Grapple 2	Malden Island Pacific	31 May 1957	Megaton	Air dropped – high air burst over ocean
Grapple 3	Malden Island Pacific	19 Jun 1957	Megaton	Air dropped – high air burst over ocean
Antler	Maralinga (Tadje)	14 Sep 1957	1 kt	Tower mounted
Antler	Maralinga (Biak)	25 Sep 1957	6 kt	Tower mounted

Code	Location	Date	Yield Range	Explosion Conditions
Antler	Maralinga (Taranaki)	9 Oct 1957	25 kt	Balloon suspended – high air burst over land
Grapple X	Christmas Island	8 Nov 1957	Megaton	Air dropped – high air burst over ocean
Grapple Y	Christmas Island	28 Apr 1958	Megaton	Air dropped – high air burst over ocean
Grapple Z	Christmas Island	22 Aug 1958	Kiloton	Balloon suspended – air burst over land
Grapple Z	Christmas Island	2 Sep 1958	Megaton	Air dropped – high air burst over ocean
Grapple Z	Christmas Island	11 Sep 1958	Megaton	Air dropped – high air burst over ocean
Grapple Z	Christmas Island	23 Sep 1958	Kiloton	Balloon suspended – high air burst over land

Kiloton (i.e. a thousand tons of TNT) – yield range (1–1000 kiloton)
Megaton (i.e. a million tons of TNT) – yield range (few hundred kiloton to several megaton)

This table is as published by the Ministry of Defence, London.

APPENDIX III

BRITISH NUCLEAR TESTS VETERANS ASSOCIATION
Chairman: Mr Ken McGinley

Pitcairlie House,
East Bay,
Dunoon, Argyll.

BRITISH ATOMIC VETERANS ASSOCIATION
Secretary: Mr Tom Armstrong

Staddlestones,
Welford Road,
Long Marston,
Stratford-upon-Avon,
CV37 8RA